Exploration in Art:

The Journey of a Mother and Daughter

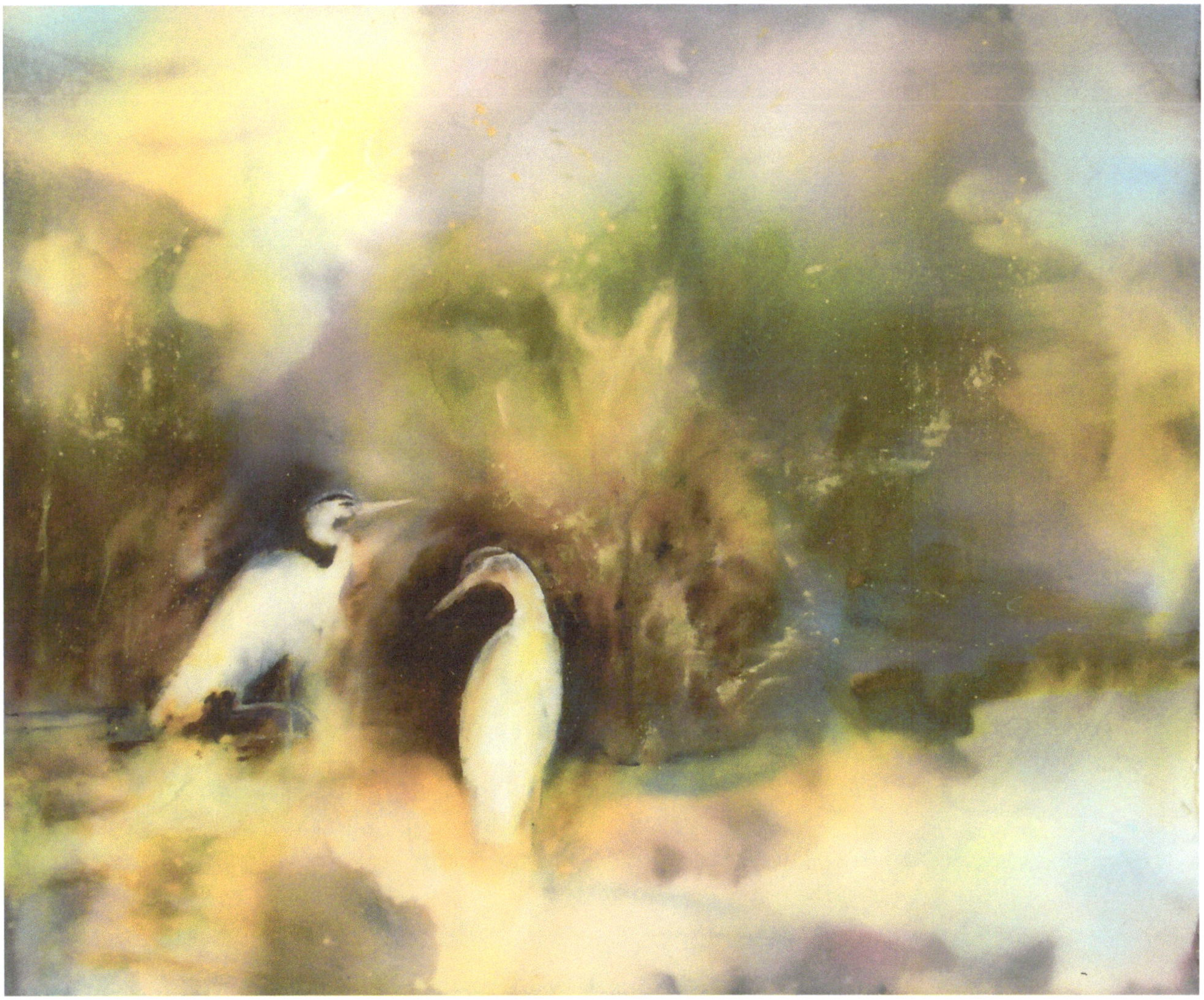

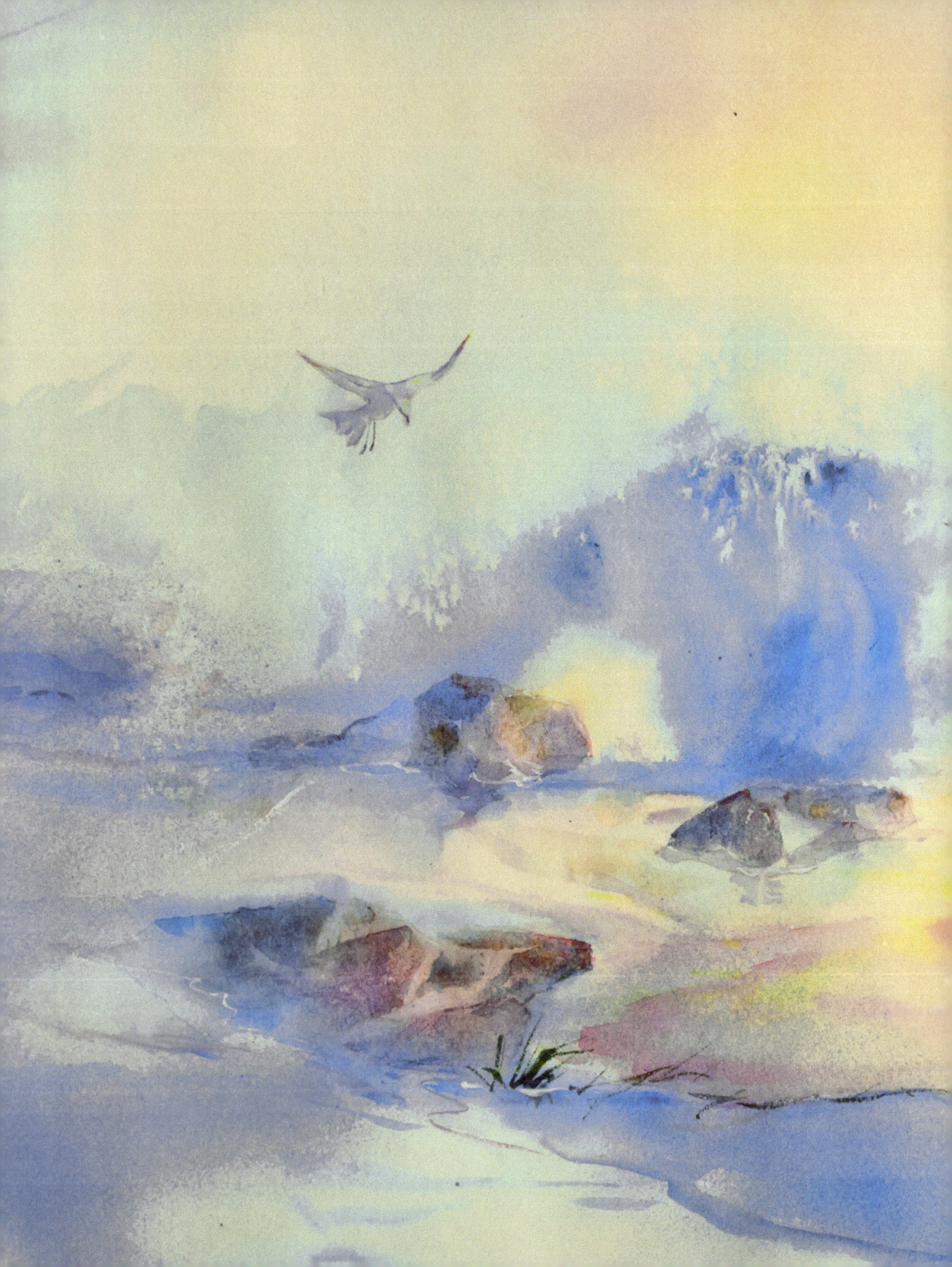

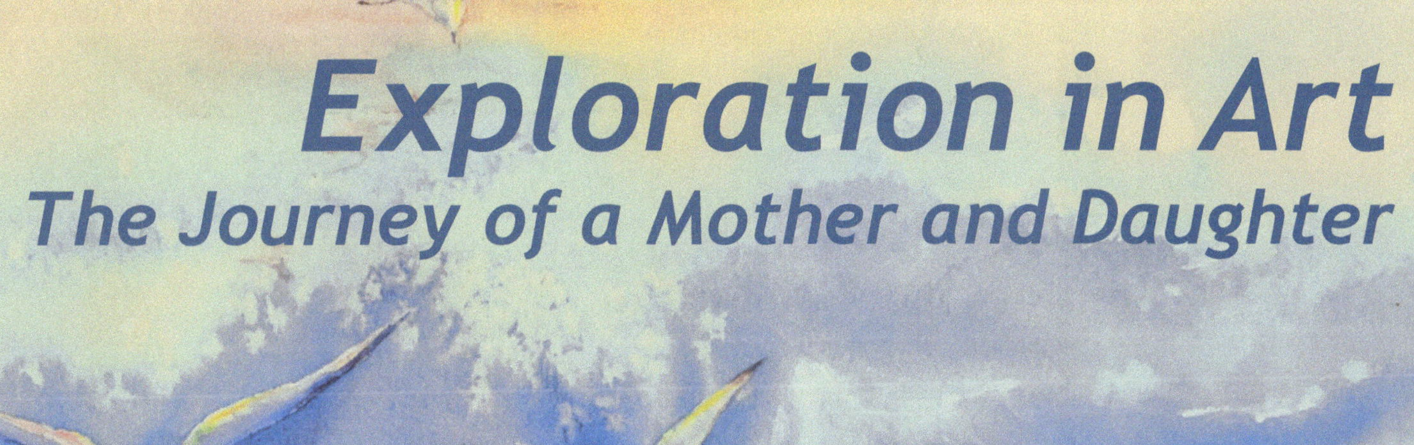

Exploration in Art

The Journey of a Mother and Daughter

Judith Bender
Anneke Bender

Acknowledgments

I gratefully acknowledge the following artists for the generosity of their teaching and the beautiful exhibition of their work: fabric artist, Evelyn Unger; watercolorists, Karlyn Holman, Tom Lynch, Jeanne Carbonetti and Nita Engle. The work of each has lead me beyond the realm of artistic techniques into an amazing, tender, and beautiful world view. I am also grateful for the generosity and artistic expertise of Gerry Weber and Mikel Darling, who photographed the paintings for this book. My gratitude goes to Zora Ugolini Herr and Cindy Johnson for our past explorations in healing energy and our continuing participation with each other in this unique and mysterious journey.

To my husband Don who always supports our work in painting and poetry and built those early morning stove fires to warm my painting space. I appreciate the constant encouragement of my son Chris, who seems to understand what I am saying in the paintings. May we continue to learn from his sons, Brandon and Pierce, who teach us playfulness.

Judith Bender

I am forever grateful to Gerry Weber, whose companionship makes for a thoroughly joyful and interesting life, and whose photographs are contained in this book. To my Dad, whose unwavering belief in me has followed me through all my years, both turbulent and content. Thanks to my Mom, who always got my poetry and encouraged me to write more, and whose influence can be seen clearly on these pages. To Mary Oliver and Carolyn Forché, whose poetry I deeply love, who have both taught me how poetry can capture and magnify life in such an exquisite way. I finally and gratefully acknowledge all those who stand up in front of crowds and read their poetry or show their art or in any way put themselves center stage for the courage it requires, and the gift it then provides.

Anneke Bender

Published by *Producciones de la Hamaca*, Caye Caulker, Belize

ISBN: 978-976-8142-27-6

All paintings were photographed either by Gerald Weber or Mikel Darling.

The painting on the cover and title page is "Playful Mood" by Judith Bender.

The painting on the frontspiece is "Two Egret" by Judith Bender.

Producciones de la Hamaca is dedicated to:

—Celebration and documentation of Earth and all her inhabitants,

—Restoration and conservation of Earth's natural resources,

—Creative expression of the sacredness of Earth and Spirit.

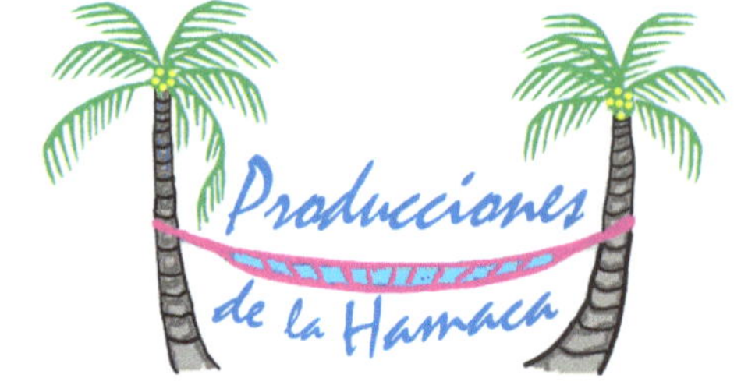

Contents

*Paintings are in regular type.
**Poems are in Italics.

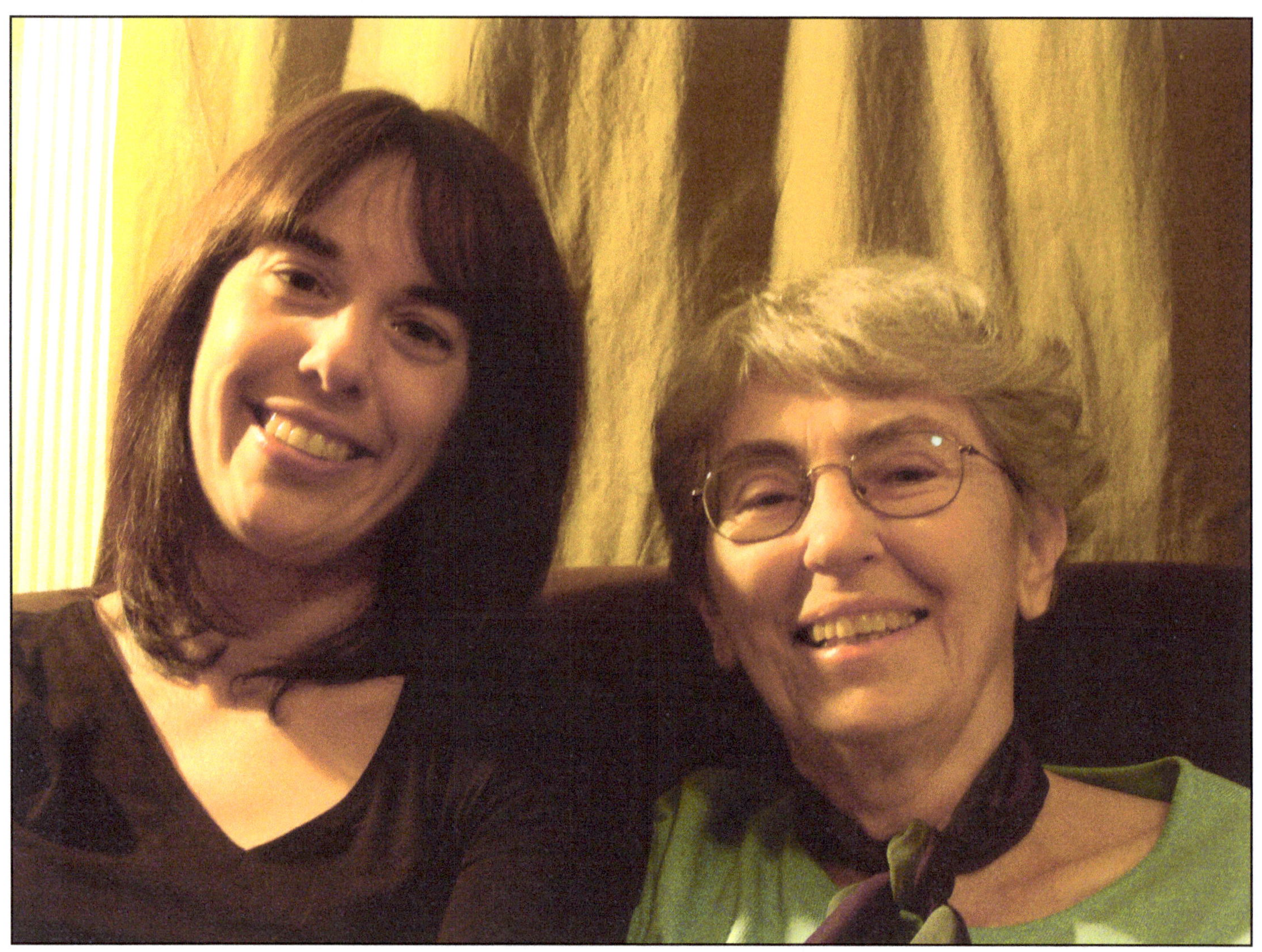

Mother-Daughter Creative Ventures

The inspiration for this book was to explore our unique and common creative processes as mother and daughter. We have always been interested in each other's creative journeys and encouraged each other through the years. As we grew older and somewhat more accomplished, we became more involved in reviewing each other's work. Although our world views are not identical, as different generations seldom are, working together has given us a great capacity to understand and deeply appreciate the contrasts and similarities in our beliefs. Because these thoughts, feelings, and attitudes that are uniquely expressed in our art—painting and poetry—underlie the practical basis for our everyday lives, we have found that we continually grow in understanding and appreciation of each other.

In our view, the poems presented with paintings relate in some way, usually by image or mood. Few of the paintings or poems were produced specifically to match any particular piece—we simply recognized relationships among the various pieces as we reviewed their content.

One thing you will find common in our work is a love of nature and the way in which our human lives are inter-woven within its larger fabric. An awareness of the rhythms of the natural world allows for a deeper understanding of loss and the passage of time, the basic surrender that all creatures are inextricably bound to. A sense of peace and hope arises naturally for both of us in the exploration of this oneness, and has, in turn, arisen as the central theme of our book.

Painting by Judith Bender

Personal Approach to Painting

Like most painters, I try to express my personal worldview in my work. The first painting of the book, "Bountiful Earth" (*p.1*) summarizes my thoughts, feelings, and defining beliefs about the caring Earth, particularly its oneness, its endless giving and the infusion of energy from some mysterious source. In this painting, the new birth embryo emerges from the body of Earth and is sustained in the ocean by branches that reach out from the trees.

My underlying belief, which gives artistic structure to the idea of oneness, is that Earth itself has its own gestalt consciousness. Thus, the plant and animal kingdoms of Earth are not so separate, as I had once assumed, but actually possess a certain kind of consciousnes—a presence and awareness of their beautiful and gracious cooperation.

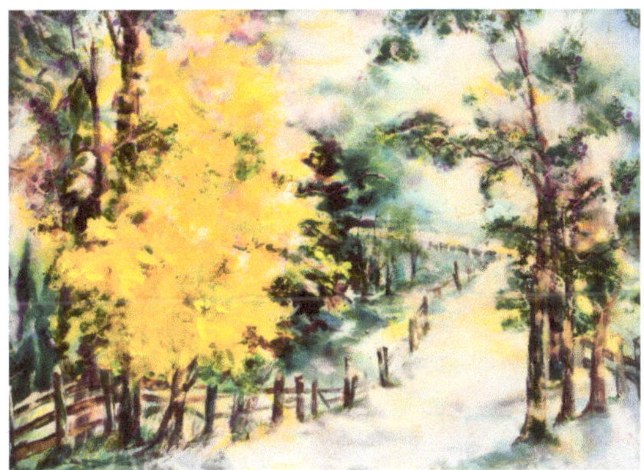

Trees Reaching for Each Other

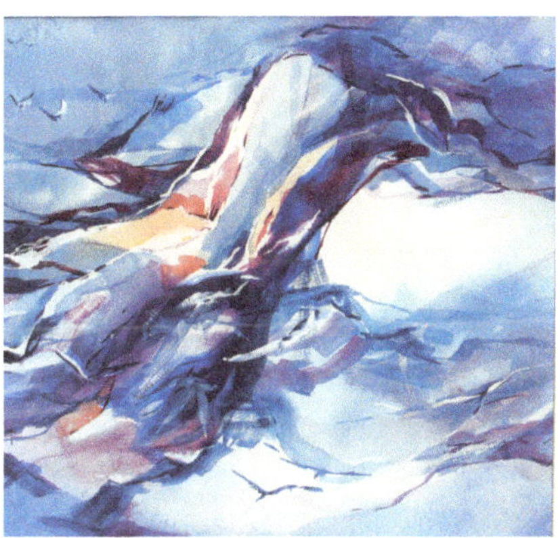

Birds Circling Mountain Glacier

In most paintings I try to continue these themes with various Earth images. For example, the secret, mysterious communication among members of Earth kingdoms might be illustrated by "Trees Reaching for Each Other (*p. 48*), the birds becoming part of the very structure of the mountain glacier in "Birds Circling Mountain Glacier" (*p. 42*), and the sunflower reaching for the bee while Earth looks on in "Invitation by the Sunflower" (*p. 2*).

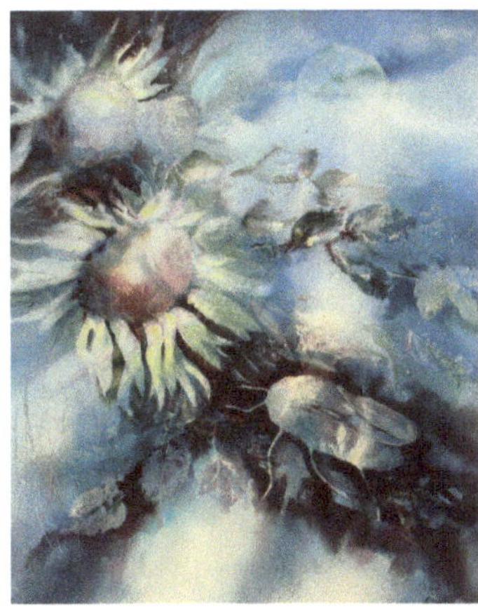

Invitation by the Sunflower

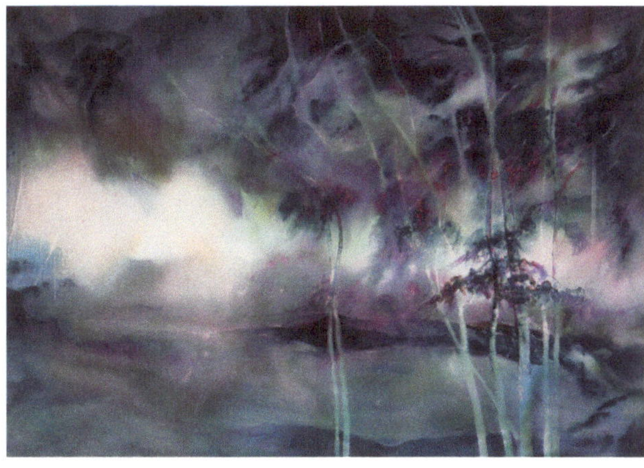

Peace and Turbulence Among the Trees

Surprising discoveries of relationships sometimes emerged during the painting process. In "Peace and Turbulence Among the Trees" (*p. 40*), the trees move through an atmosphere of storm and peace at the same time, thereby describing the landscape of our own human emotions in a compassionate awareness. It is my hope that these symbolic images in some way express the fundamental oneness that tenderly embraces all Earth kingdoms, as well as the very structures of Earth itself.

Painting by Judith Bender (cont'd)

Media and Technique

My initial approach to painting was the study of watercolor applied to dry paper and canvas according to the methods of several very knowledgeable and generous art teachers who are listed in the Acknowledgements. Because of the element of surprise and the need to sacrifice control in wet-on-wet techniques, this method became a watercolor favorite of mine. The process continues to dominate my work with fabrics and multi-media applications. I find that brush painting of dyes on wet fabric produces surprising and uncontrollable flow patterns, which become loose designs upon which to build. Seeing and recognizing the emerging pattern continually challenges my observation, focus, and internal listening. Although I generally start with an idea and even a drawing, the painting tends to have a mind of its own!

Painting on fabric is quite a unique process because the degree of flow can be adjusted by the wetness of the fabric and finished painted areas can be lightened with diluted bleach. Pigment flow can be eliminated by adding fabric gels to the concentrated dyes. Painting areas with or without gels can achieve the important variety of hard and soft lines or flow fade-out regions with clear, distinct areas for objects in a foreground. Machine quilting can be used to enhance the lines, make crisp edges, and create new interest in texture.

I have found the best instruction for fabric painting is experimentation and more experimentation, not being afraid to discard a "ruined" piece. I find it easier to let go of a piece that isn't working because fabric is much less expensive than watercolor paper. Dyes, because they come as concentrates or powdered pigments, are much more economical than any artist paints.

My sisters-in -law, Lourene and Ann Bender inspired my interest in collage. Lourene is an accomplished paper collage artist and Ann's beautiful quilts are works in fabric collage.

As in traditional quilting, pieces can be added and/or applied as over-lays using various methods of collage building. Collages can be worked out on paper or fabric substrates. Combining a dye-painted background with the application of collage materials has endless potential for building-observing-redoing. Over-laying with sheer organza silk creates interesting depth effects.

Healing Aspects of Art

The relationship of art to healing has been a core interest of mine, especially after working with compassionate healers like Zora Ugolini Herr and Cindy Johnson. They have affirmed my belief in the healing contributions of art, both in the creative process and in the energy of the end product. This aspect of art is occasionally discussed by those exploring healing using Earth energies.

Writing Poetry by Anneke Bender

Reading, writing and, more generally, language have always ranked among the great pleasures of my life. It is the pleasure of something being named, and named exactly, pulled from the lurking background of life into full focus. So often our thoughts, beliefs and emotional experience live underneath the surface, driving and motivating us, but beyond the reach of the conscious mind. Words can take you into that pool and lift a thing up for understanding. In the process of describing, things become known.

My relationship with writing has changed through the years into a process that is more about listening than talking. I remember on one particular vacation, I sat on the beach and decided to just write without any urge to form a coherent sentence—to allow whatever popped into my head onto the page. What followed was something altogether different and taught me that words carry meaning not only in their definition, but in their very sound and structure. It can be surprisingly pleasing to let words swing, lift, fall, tumble and land, then look at what you have. This unconscious throwing together often forms a structure and meaning more complex than one I could have planned.

This seems to be exactly the process my mom works with in her painting. While direction and choice are important, my mother and I both take the greatest pleasure from our art when it is surprising us, when we are following, waiting, trying to discern the hidden image.

That we have both, wholly on our own, developed such a similar creative process—and that our painting and writing so resemble each other in some basic way—strikes me as strange. I have often believed that my mom and I have very different views of life. It would appear, though, that there is something familiar about how we perceive the world when we let go of our intellectual framing.

I couldn't tell you why words are the tool I use, or why my mother uses painting, or why anyone uses anything in particular. Maybe you develop these preferences from your genetic wiring, or what you have been exposed to, or from who has inspired you in the course of your life. It seems to be instinctive and natural—a preferred activity through which you unlock the mystery of your life.

Writing is my way of coming to terms, as it were. The process itself has been a loyal companion through the years. And truly, I'm not sure if it's writing itself, the understandings it offers up, or the wide open space it provides. It's possible all art forms take you there, to the same pool, and the end result is just your momentary translation of what you find swimming there.

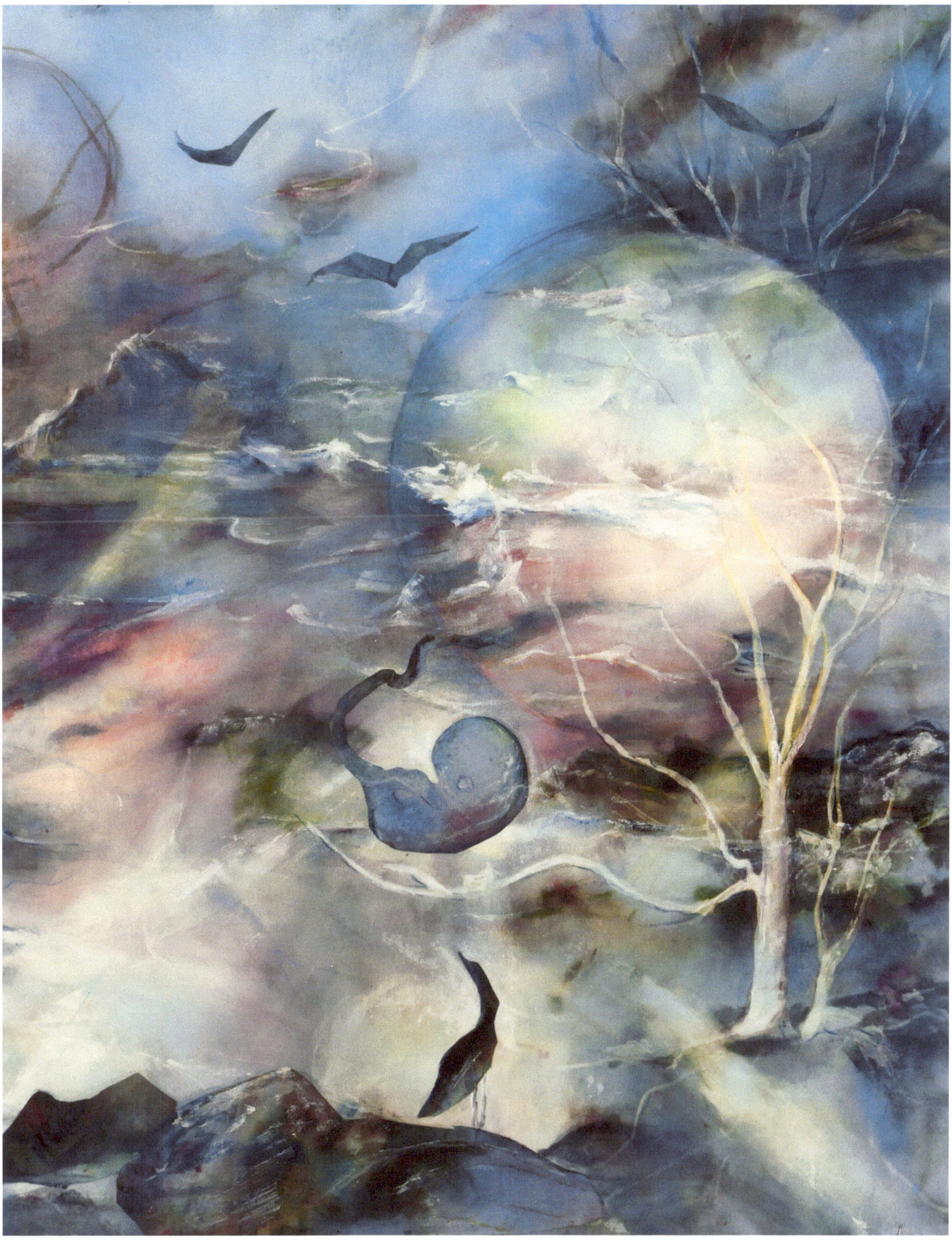

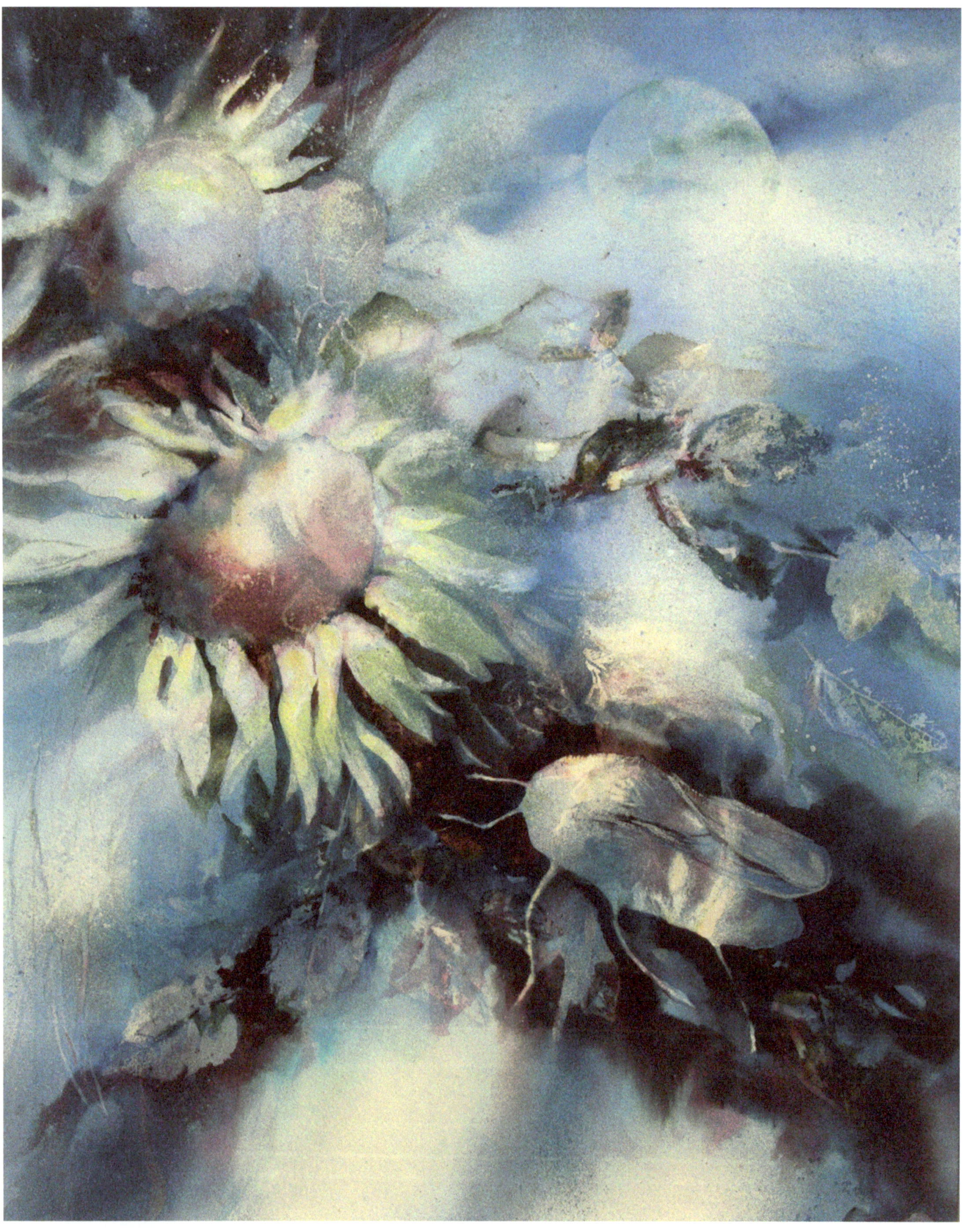

Crumbs

One still moment:
A drop of rain rolling down a cold window,
A bead of sweat dropping from an eyelash,
a piece,
   a crumb,
      of time.
God holds a hand full of crumbs—
   sweat and the cell of a bee,
   a creature's crawl,
   on it's wing a shining pinhole of sun
God holds a hand full of crumbs—
   how we all want something
   how we all stretch to touch the red hole
      the dazzling circle,
      the wild flame,
   how we all reach open mouthed, new birds for a mother's tongue.

Pulsation

A warm void, soft and dim.
Feathers that brush wind,
curling eddies flung lightly.
Folded air that wraps soft sounds.
In held breath, a pause.
Grey rocks that build soft walls,
yielding in centuries to the
persistent wailing force,
the feverish yearn of water
for a place to rest.
Gills that gather and flush, pull
and push.
In held breath, still pools of blue
glisten inside eager lungs.
There is a pulsing, a distant star
that holds its breath,
then breathes.

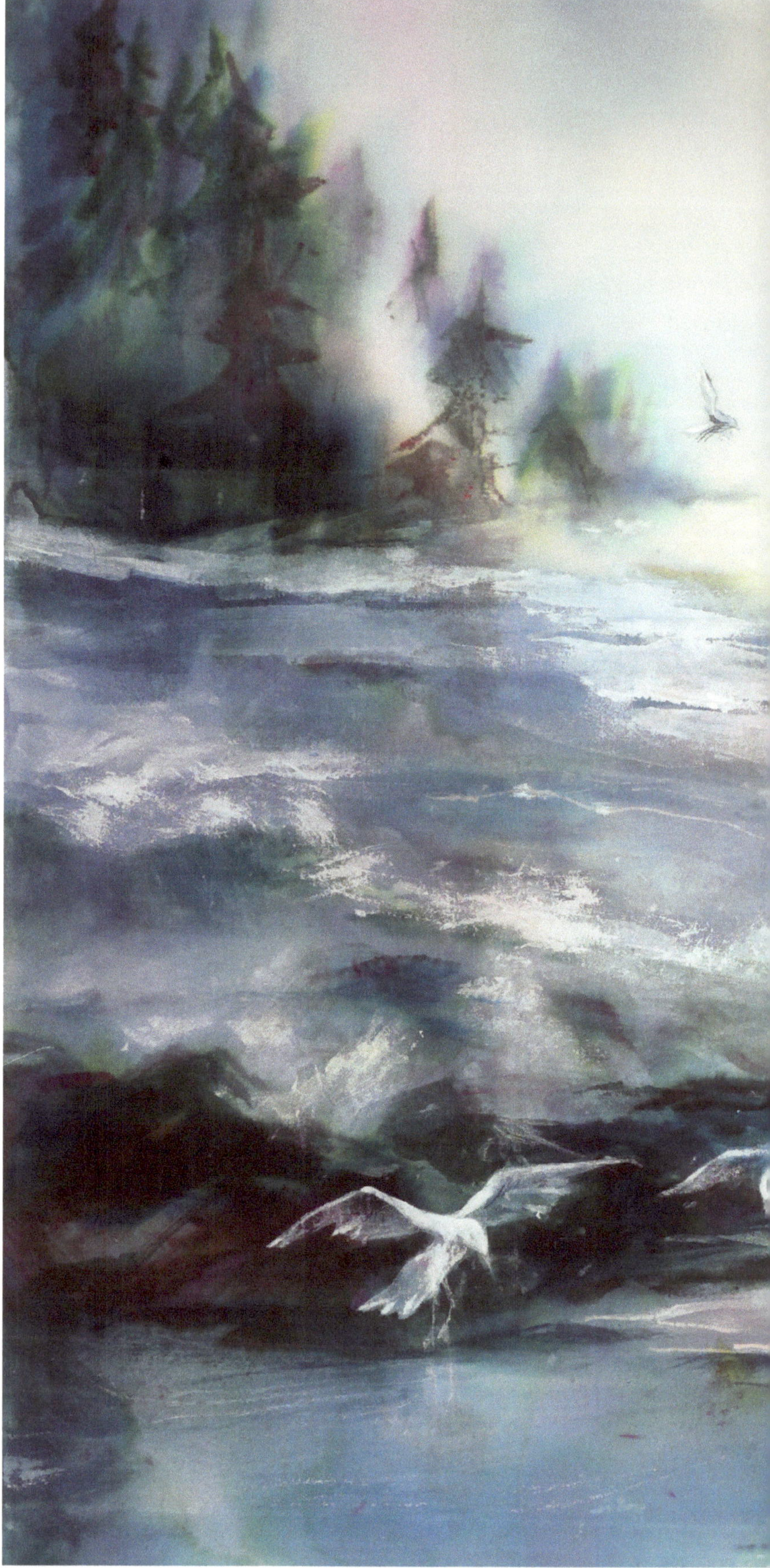

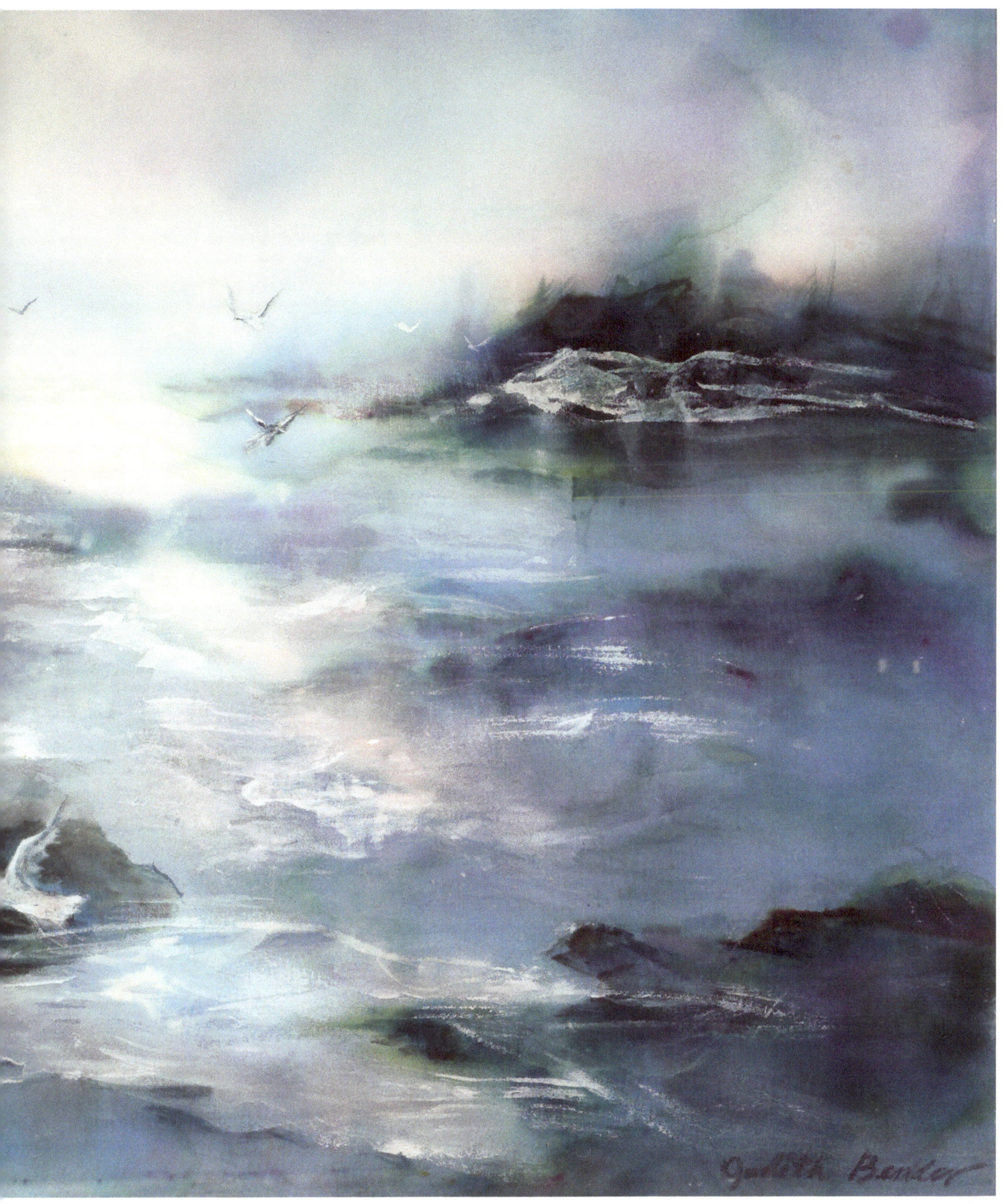

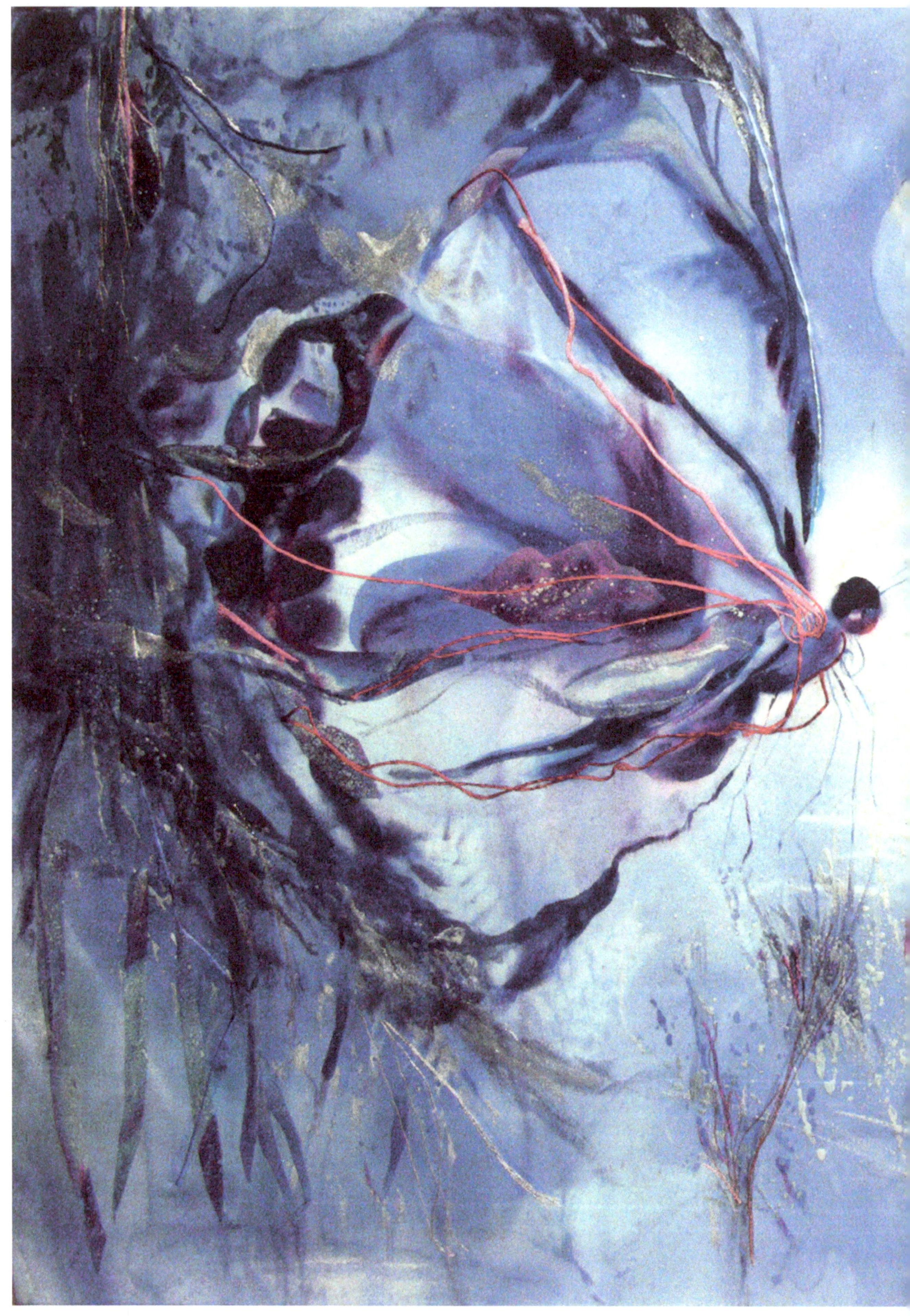

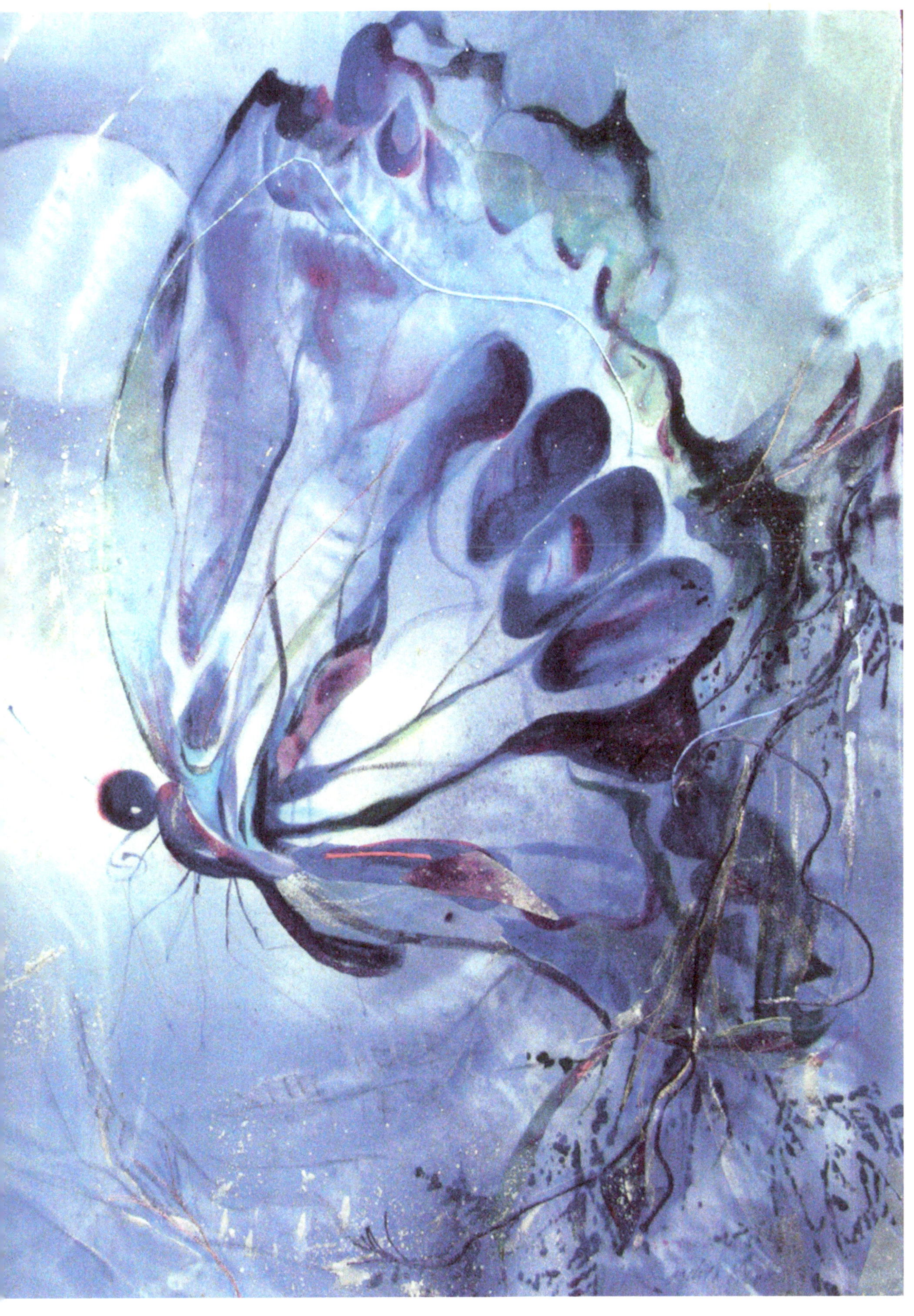

Desert

Sweat travels down caked faces,
lines of skin carved in the sprinkled crust of days.
Days roll by,
big as legend,
big as sky.
The sun fills each gentle curve of earth to the other.

Solitary vegetation,
bristling and punished,
raises defiant spikes to the sun.
Roots burrow,
seeking the shade of a deep grave.
Sound breaks
in sudden hissing, cracks, claps,
hot explosions.

Come night, the land rises,
spilling salty creatures from its clutches,
an underworld released.
Come night, the burrowed is unburrowed,
spit out onto the scorched shell of earth,
and mellowed
in the calm dim shade of the moon.

The creatures trust only the moon,
carve beetle leg lines
across cooled and stilled sand.

Funeral

I watch from behind my veil
the dizzy conversation,
colored opaque, soft
by an interception of material,
a dark drift of cloth to cloud the story.

Meanwhile the breeze plays a score
of cool touches on my skin,
and my mind follows the folding and unfolding
of air through mesh.

I will sit in this grass,
splaying toes and mixing myself
with green stalks,
draping my legs alongside
the curious legs of caterpillars.

Here I will find,
in the quaking mystery of afternoon,
under the splintering sun
as it falls through the arched green arms of still giants,
you are not lost.

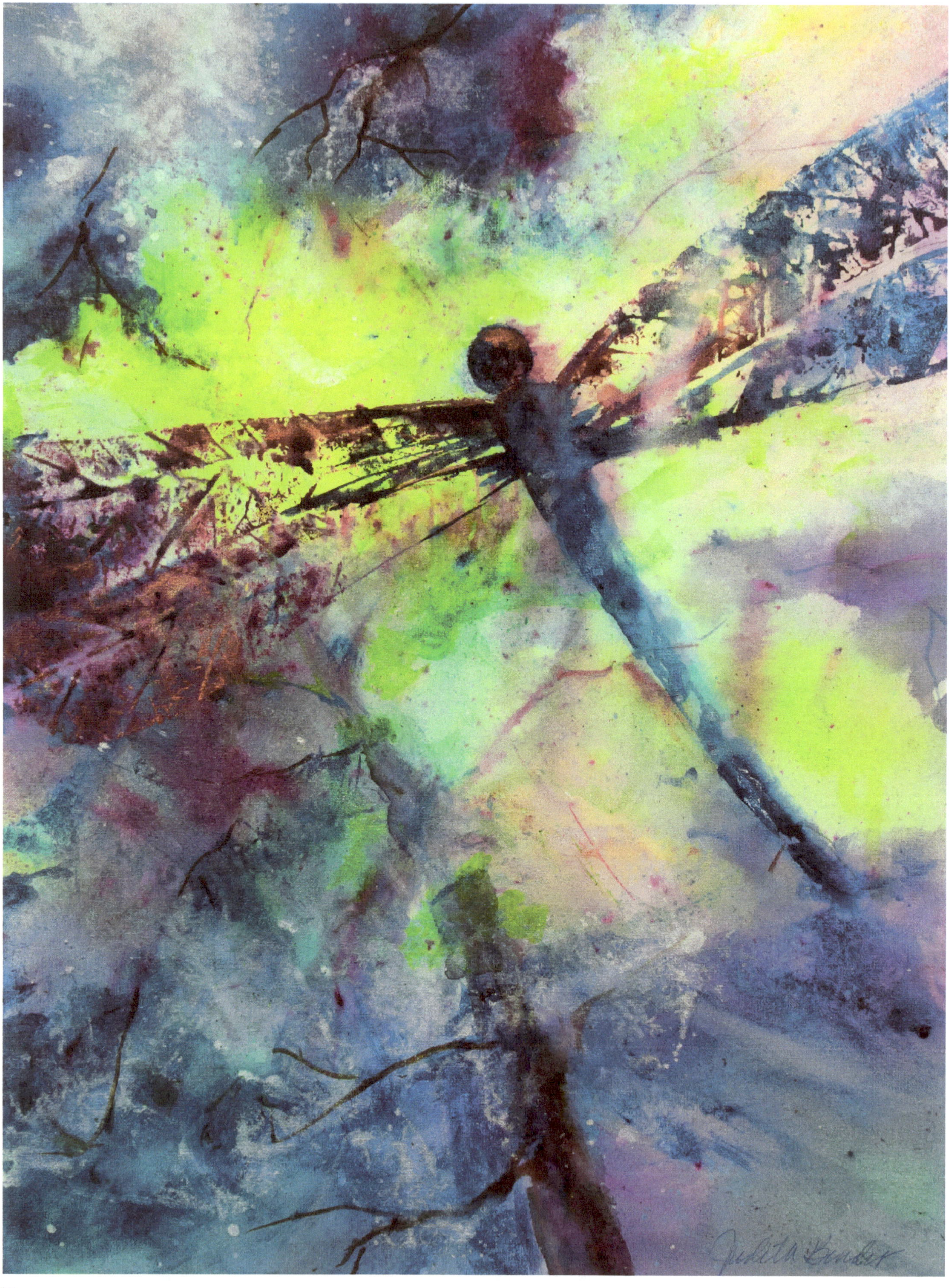

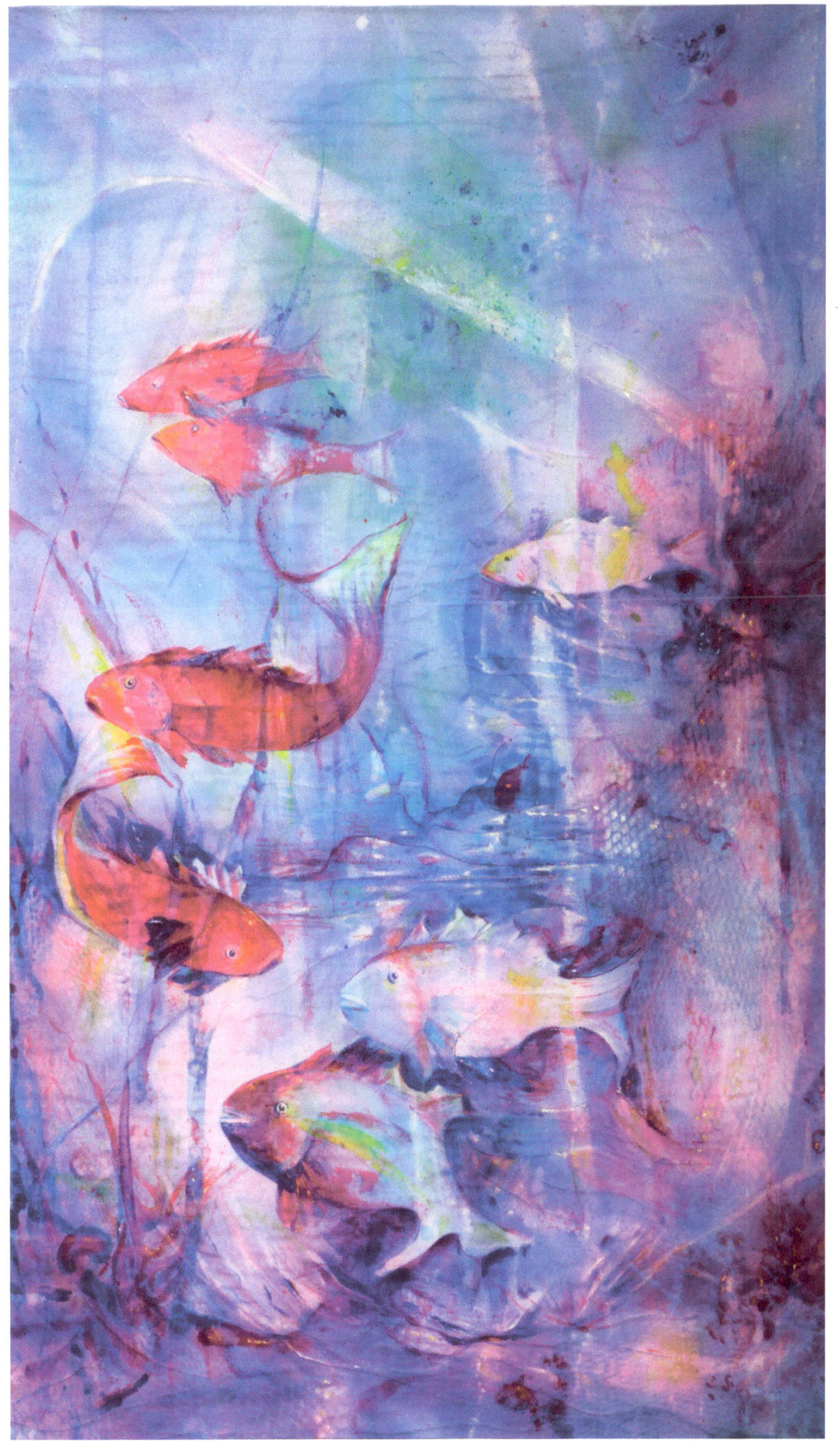

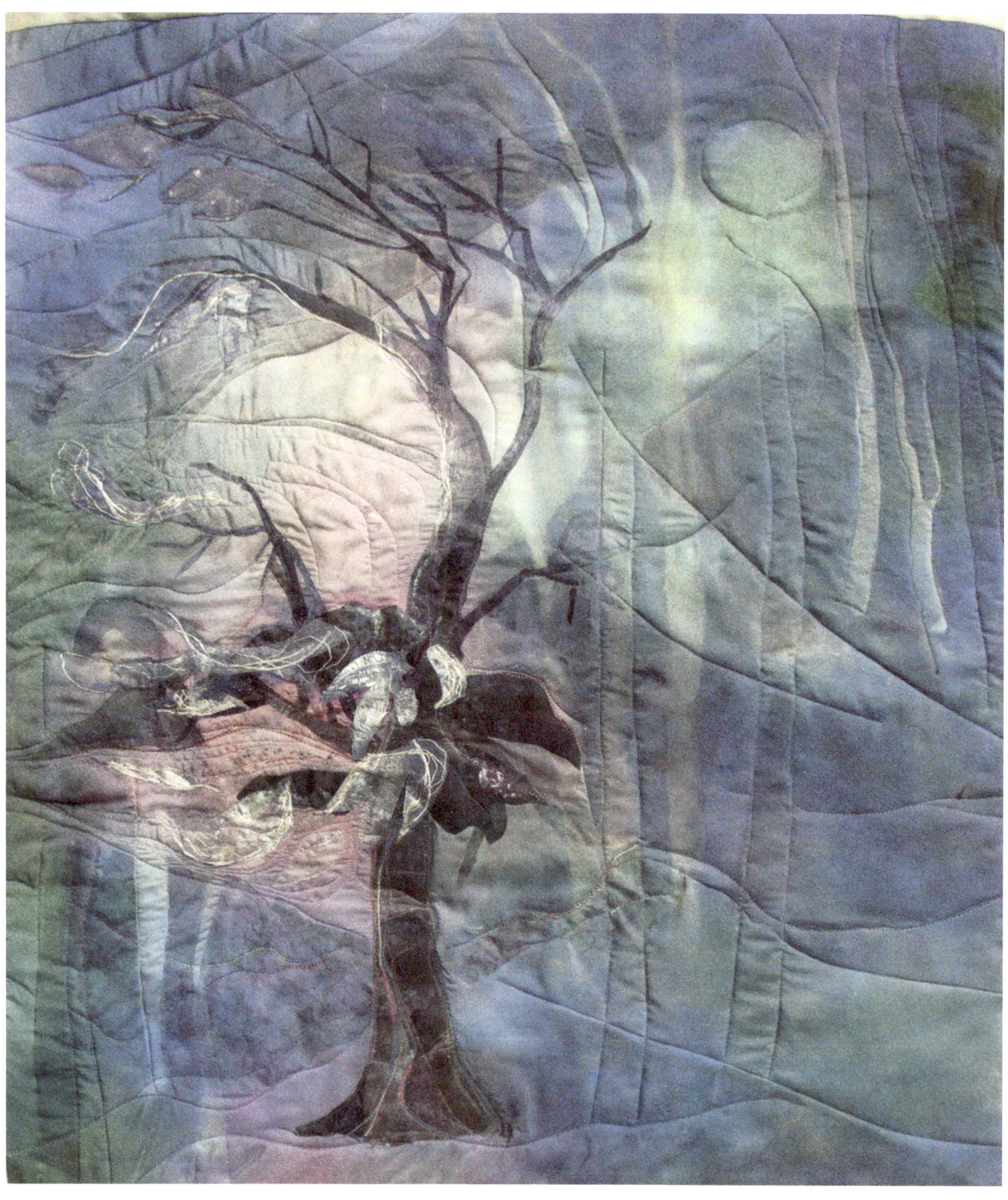

Hibernate
beneath
the winter
sky

and
remember
summer
moons.

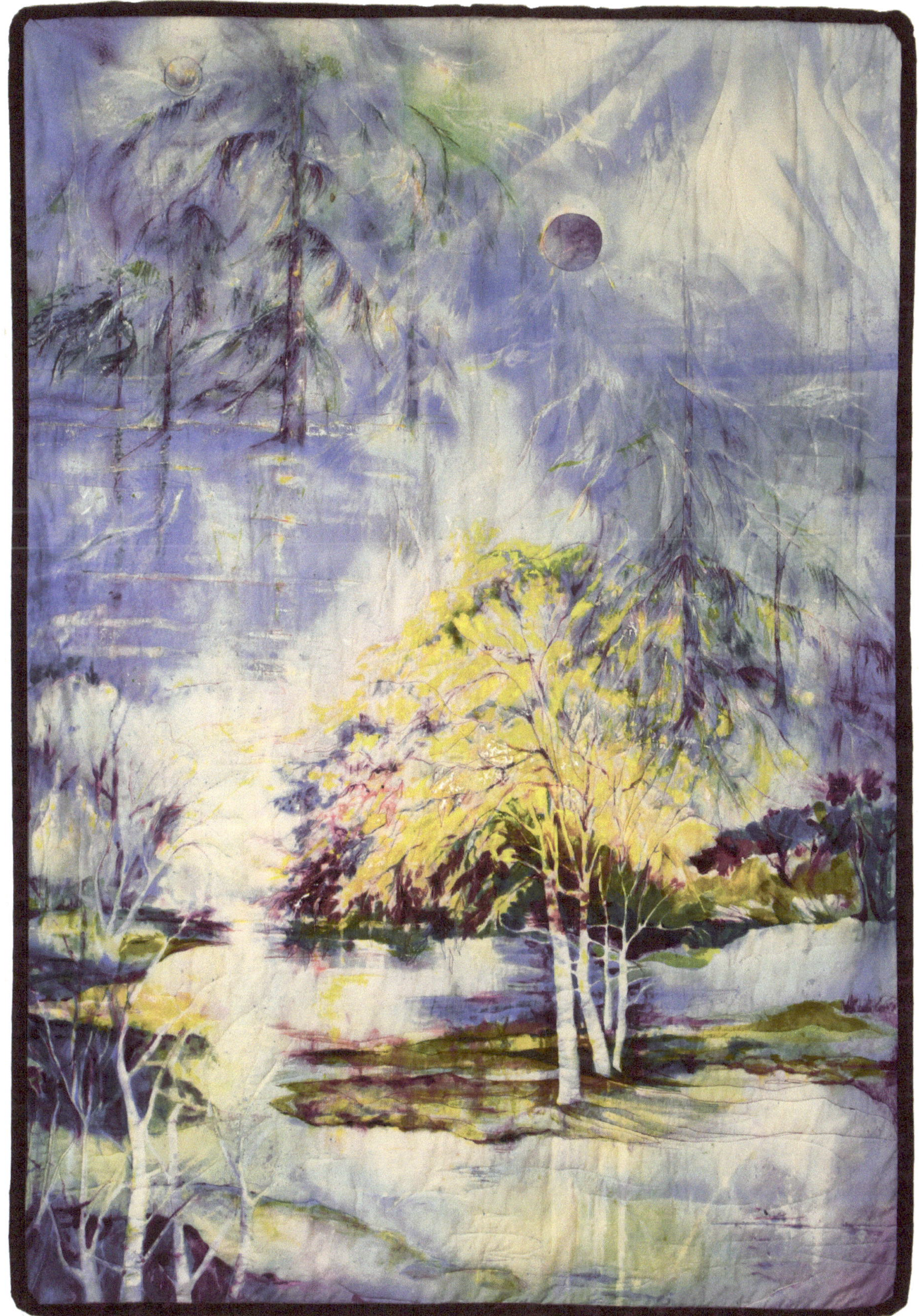

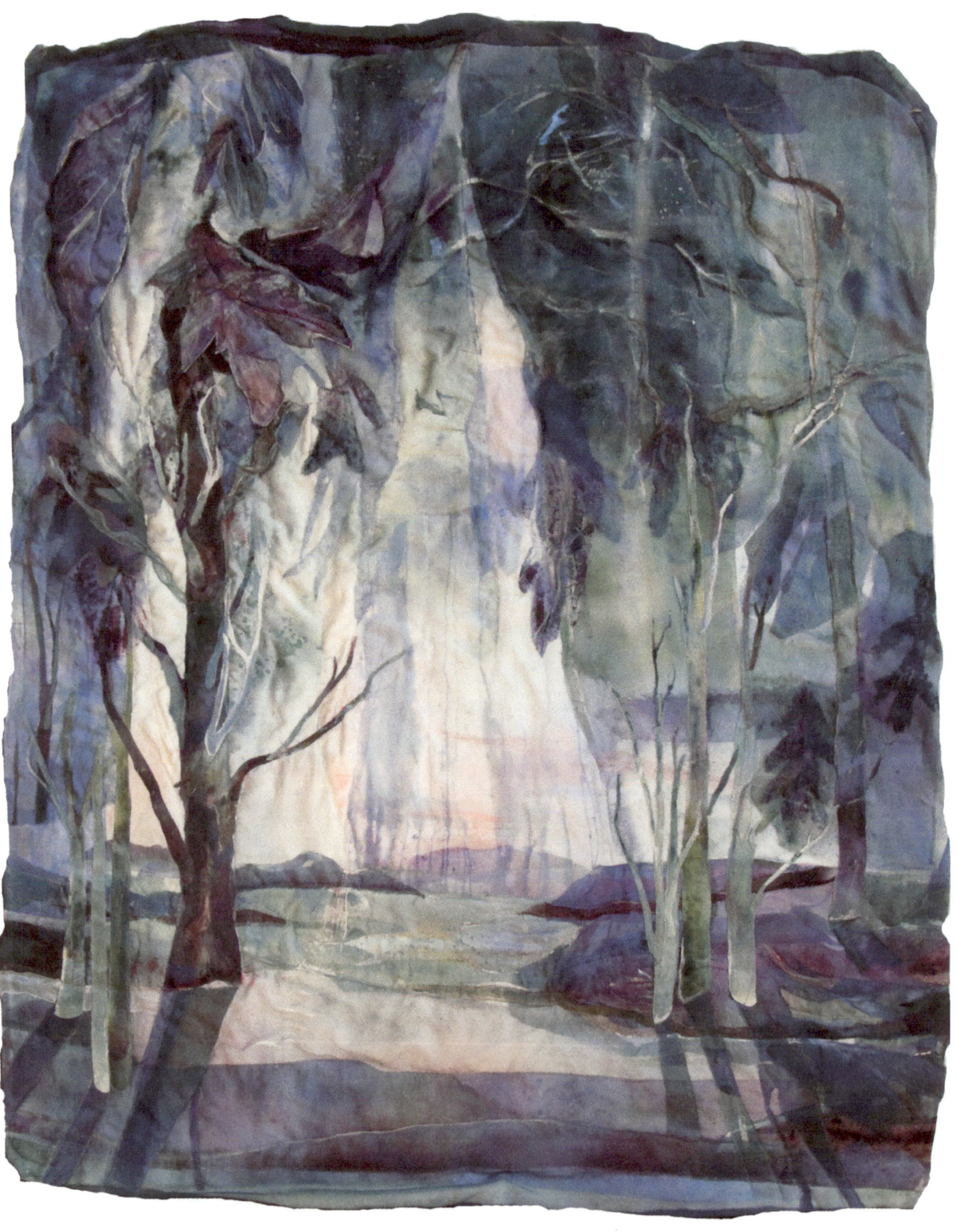

Nightlife

At night, breezes cool
the fragile veins
of leaves and wings,
soft fingers of wind
through nature's lace.
At night the moon
will swing between branches,
throw shadows,
hold a creatures' shuffling
in its silver spotlight.
There are things that belong in night.
Secrets held from those who rest.
Creatures who move by feel,
who seek
and are called.

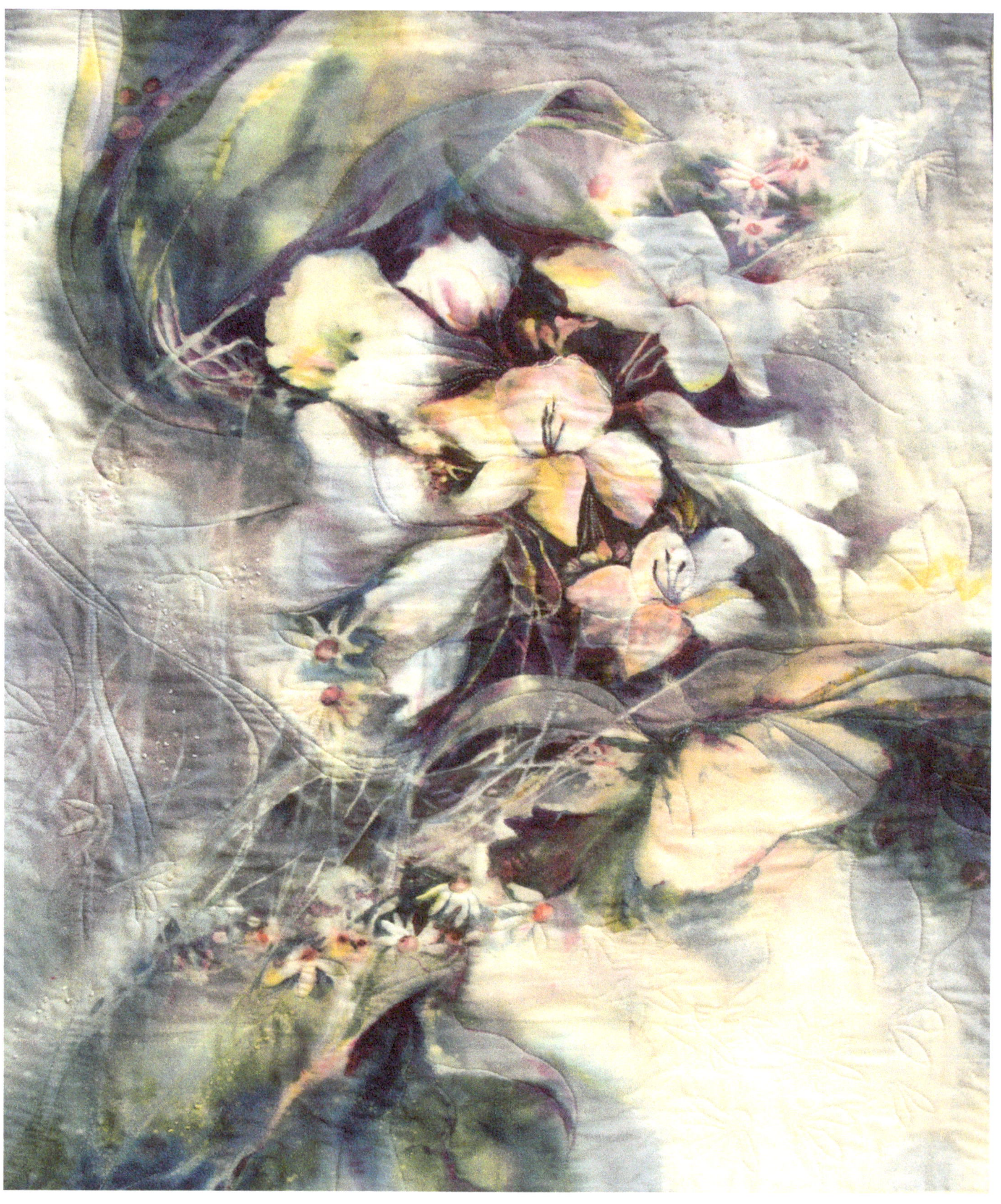

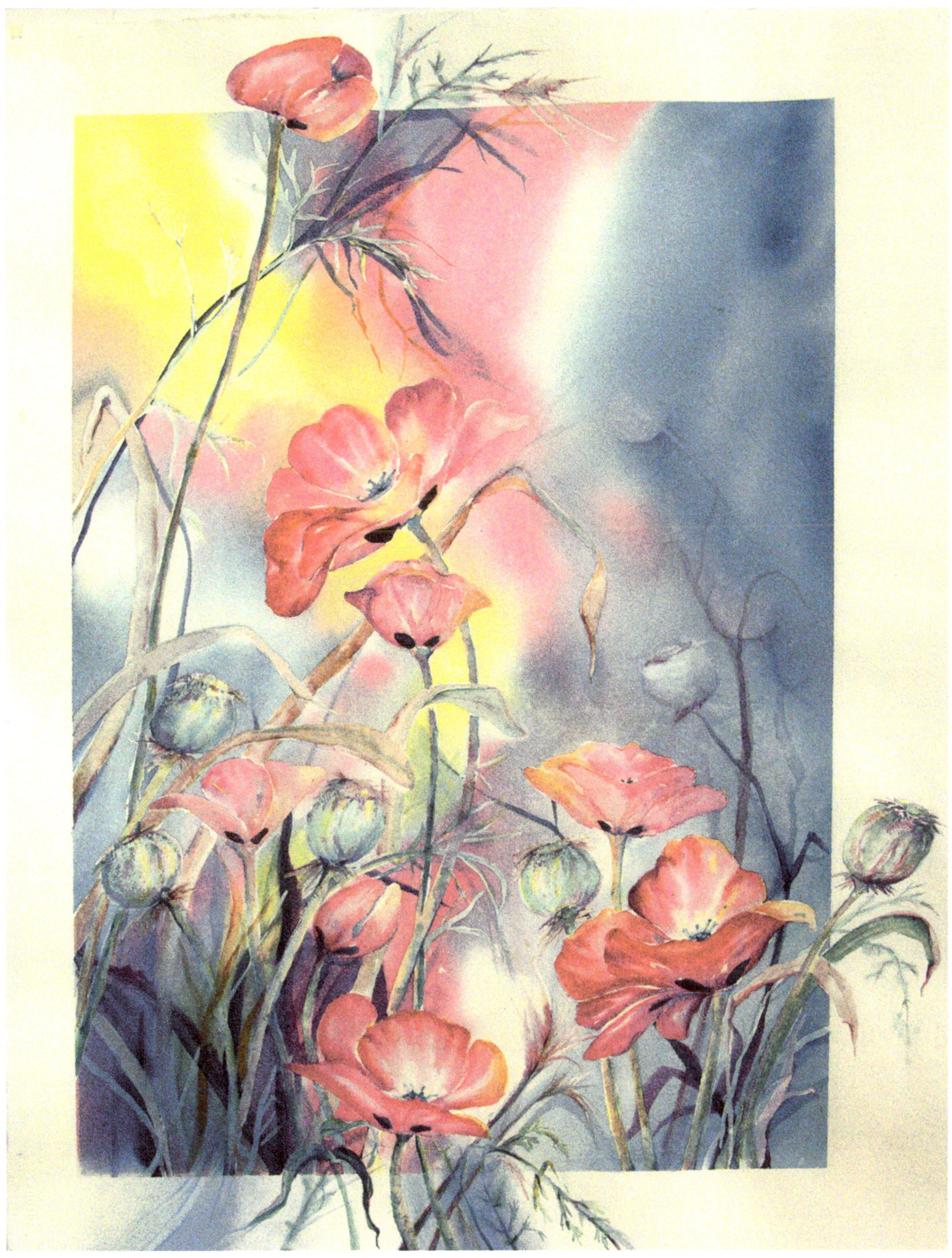

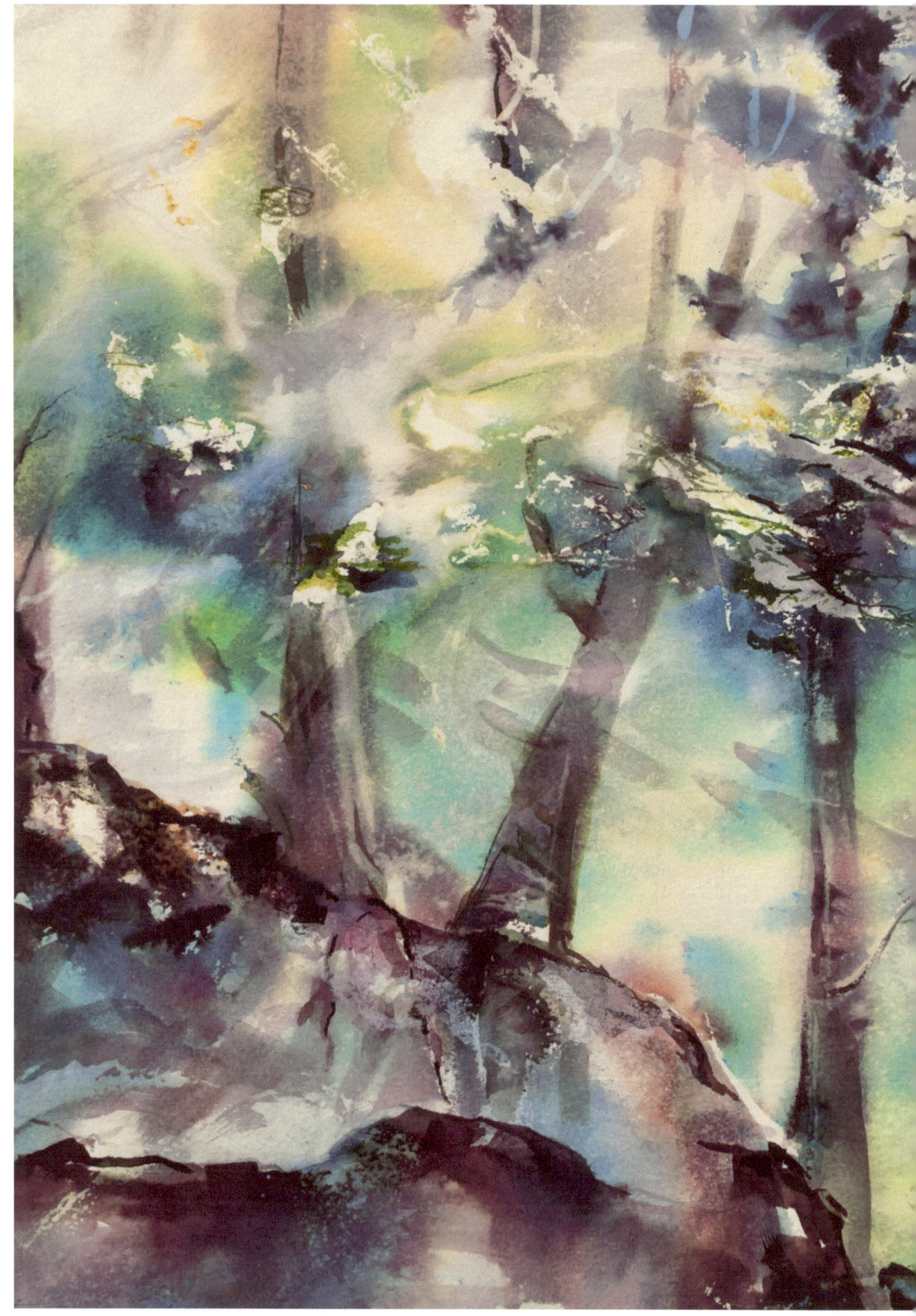

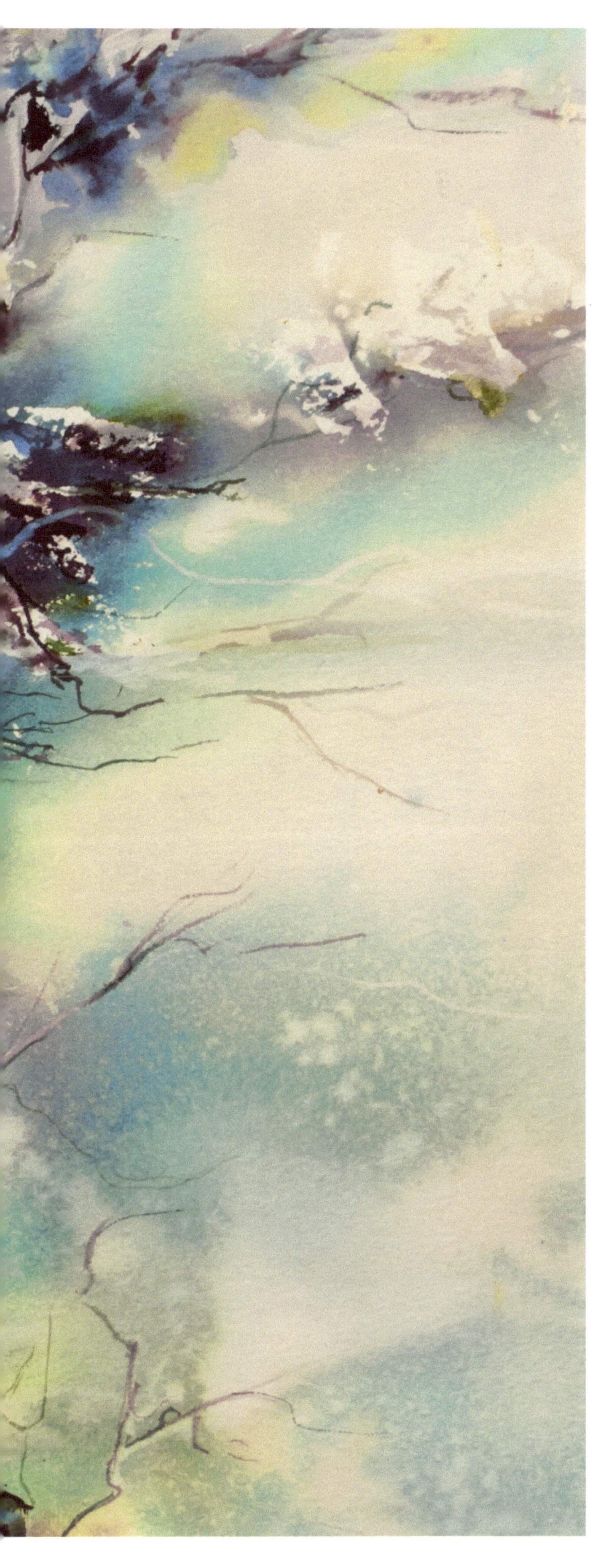

Configuration

Centuries pass in this infinite game
of wind and whispering atoms.
Each molecule falls together
in a fateful pattern—
an inevitable kiss,
a perfect melody,
the first insistent stroke of the heart.

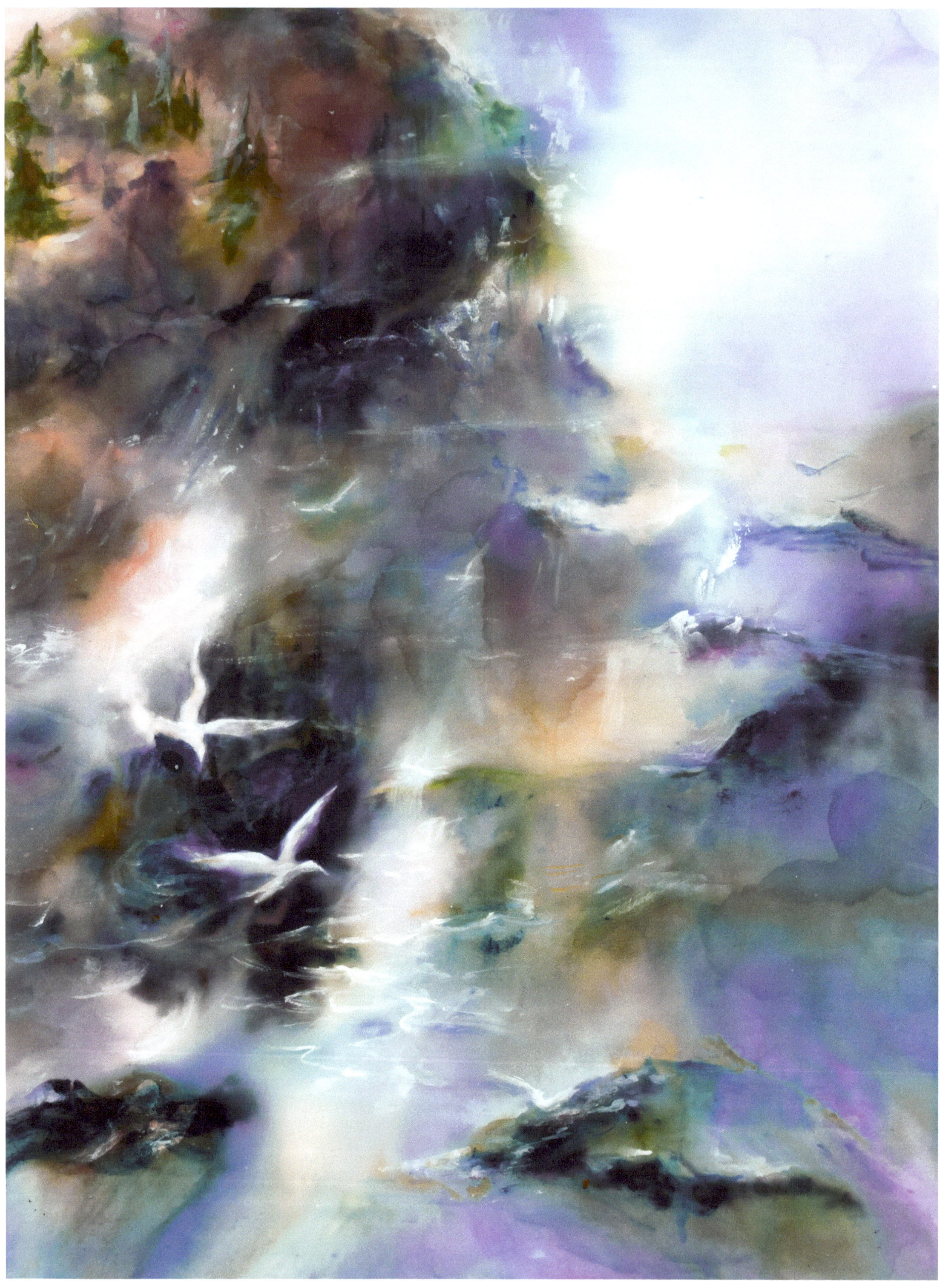

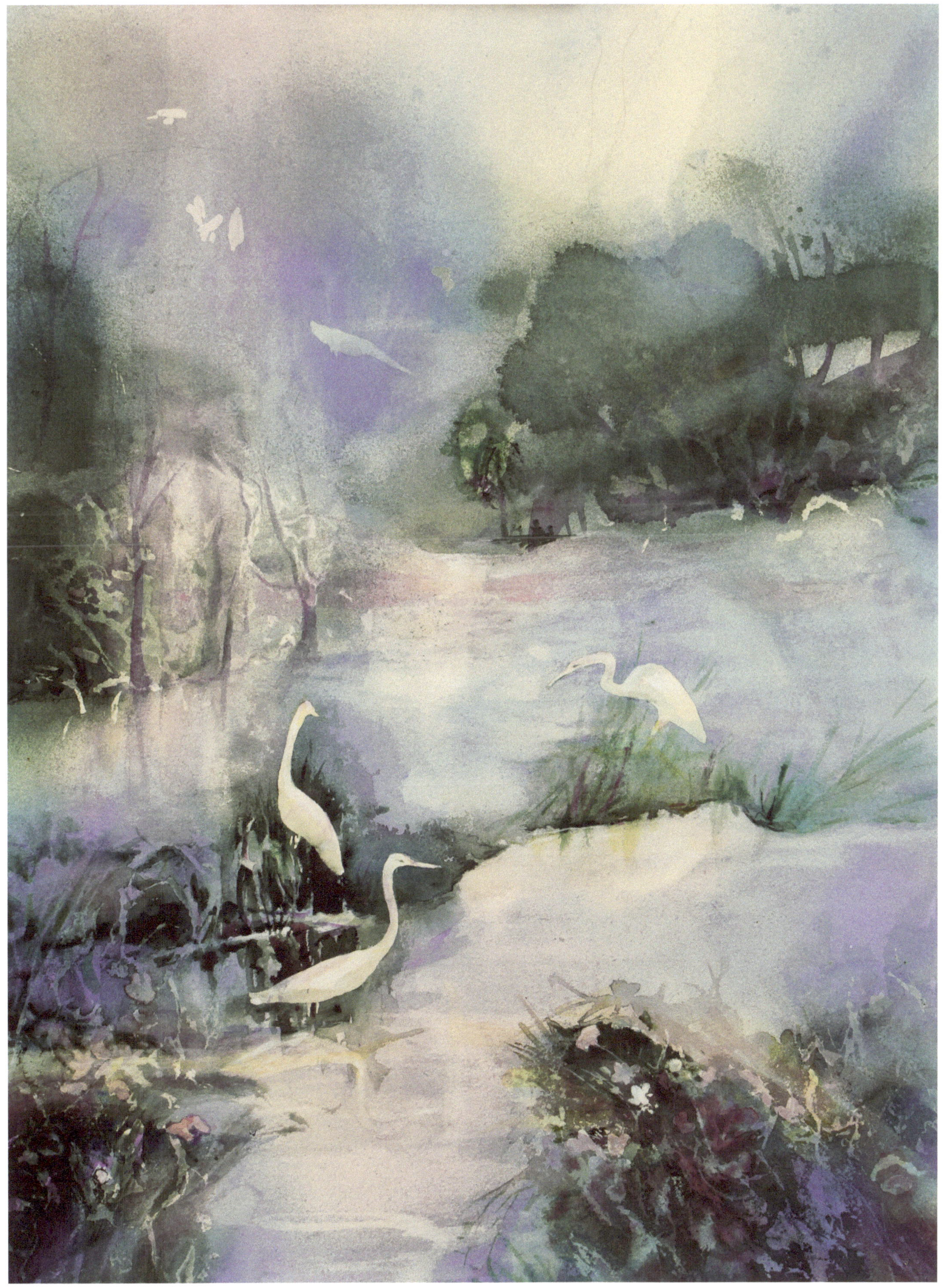

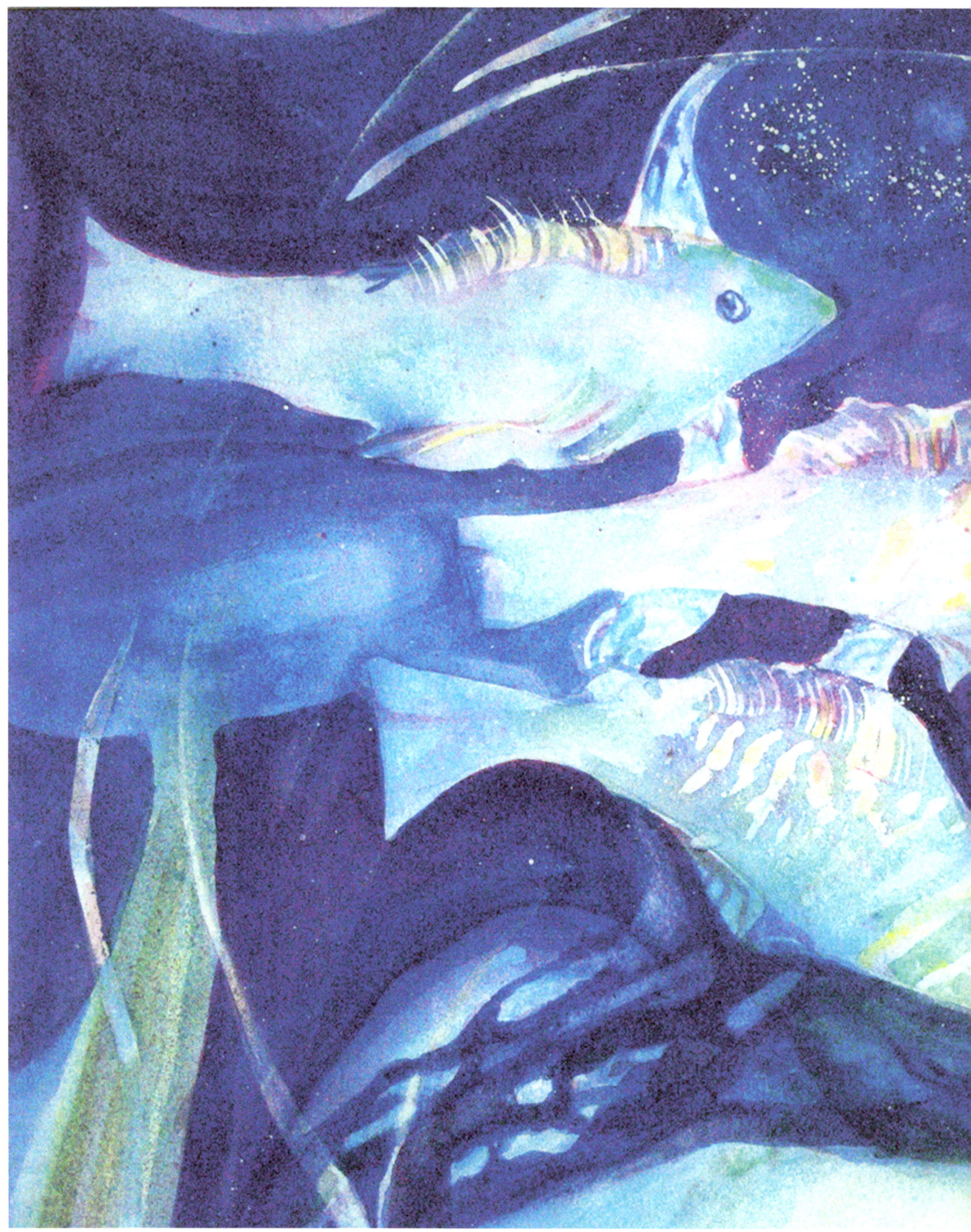

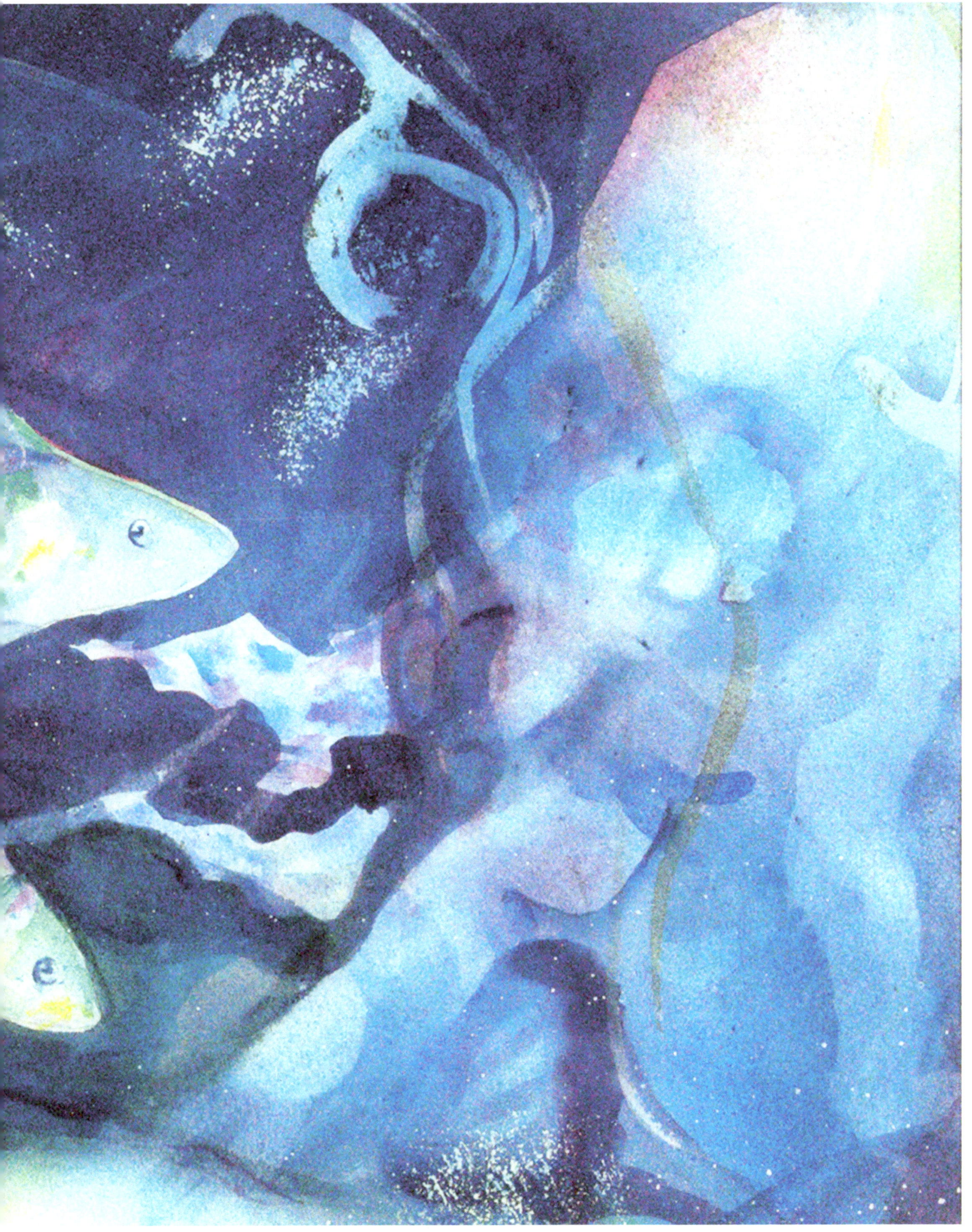

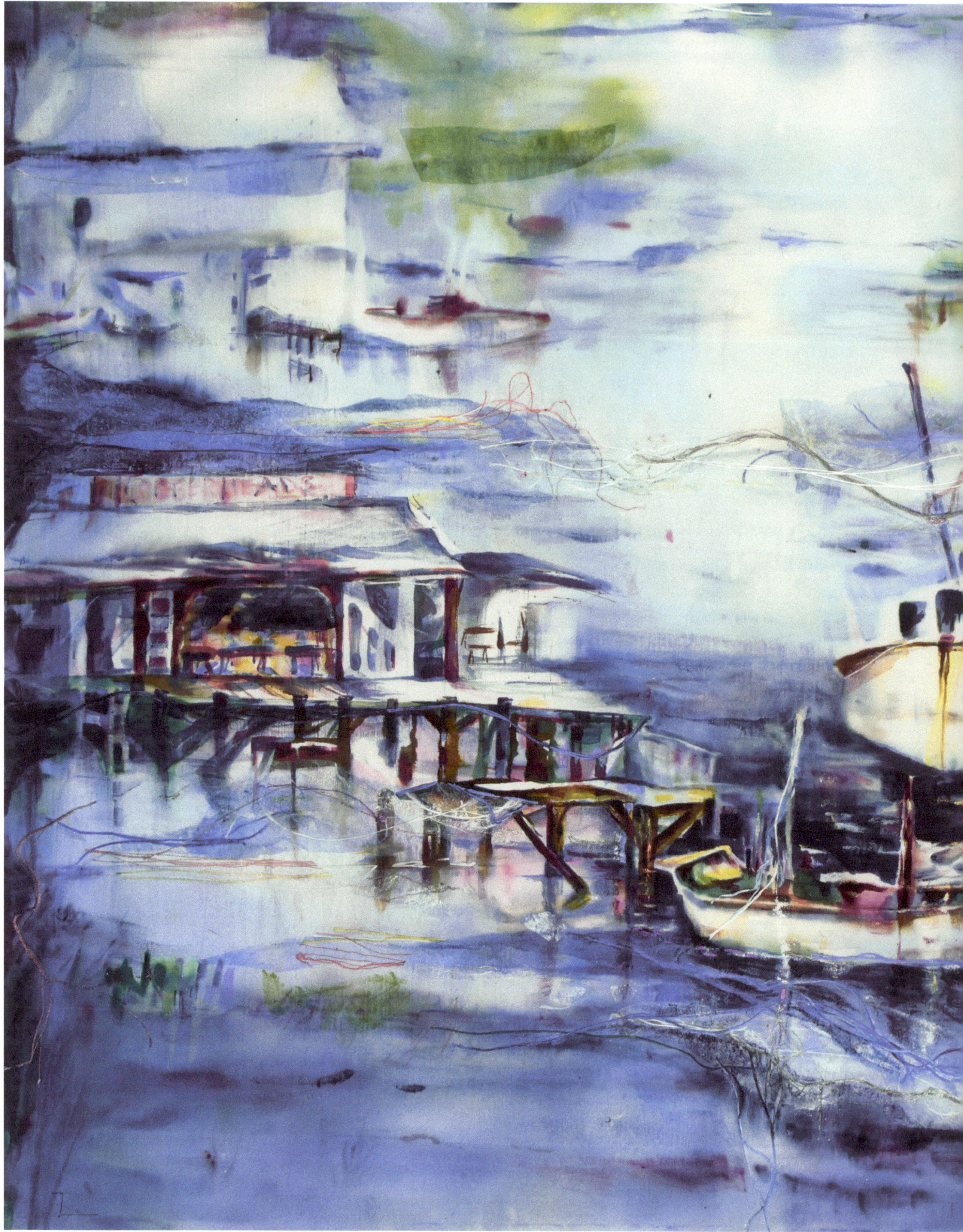

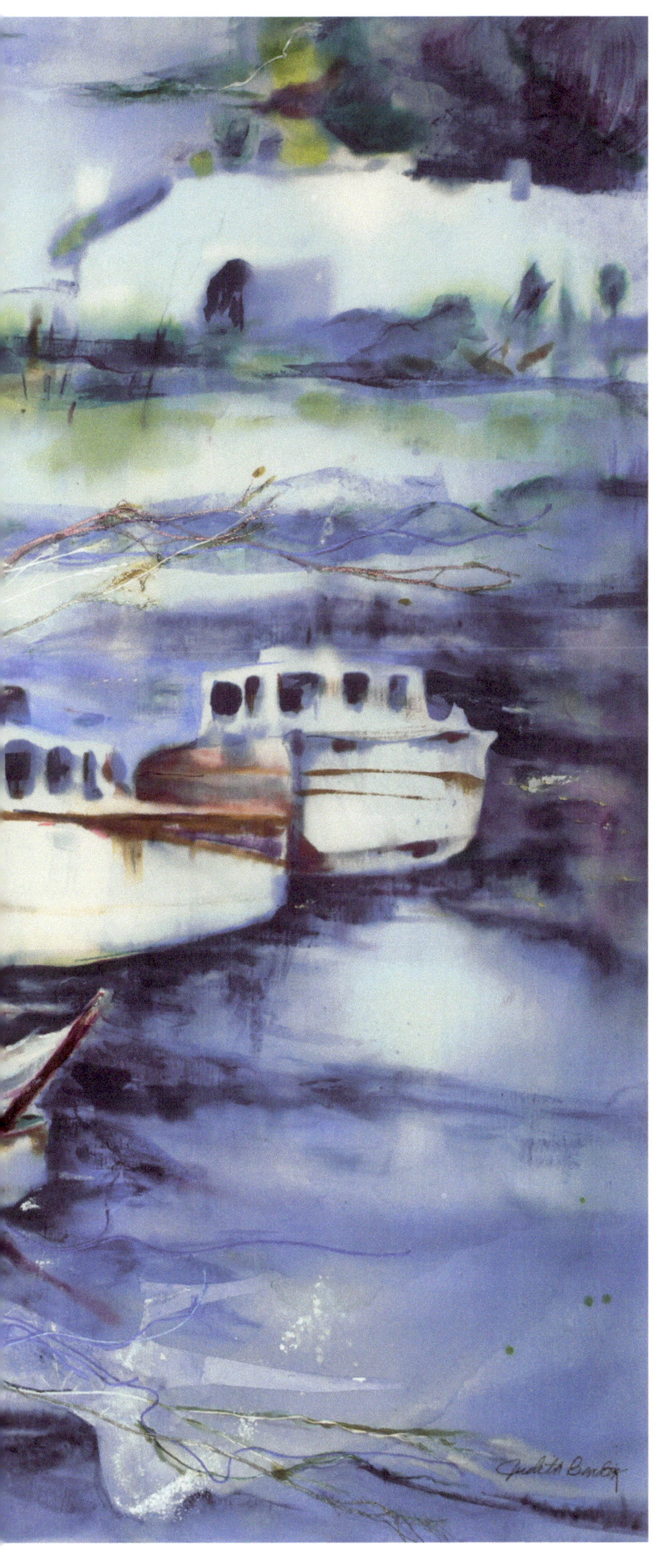

The Seam

There was a wind-torn town,
grey with mist from the sea,
with slick black rocks that cut the sky,
far call of destiny.

The souls that called this place their home
walked in paths of dream,
with beacons of clouded light ahead,
slipping through the seam.

Italy

In the piazza,
the sun holds the world
in a bright glow,
baking bricks in a slow oven,
700 years or more.
I dine on truffles.
My skin browns
under the wide open
olive sky.
Sweat rolling in mini rows
like rain on glass.
When I return,
I must tell people
about the wine.

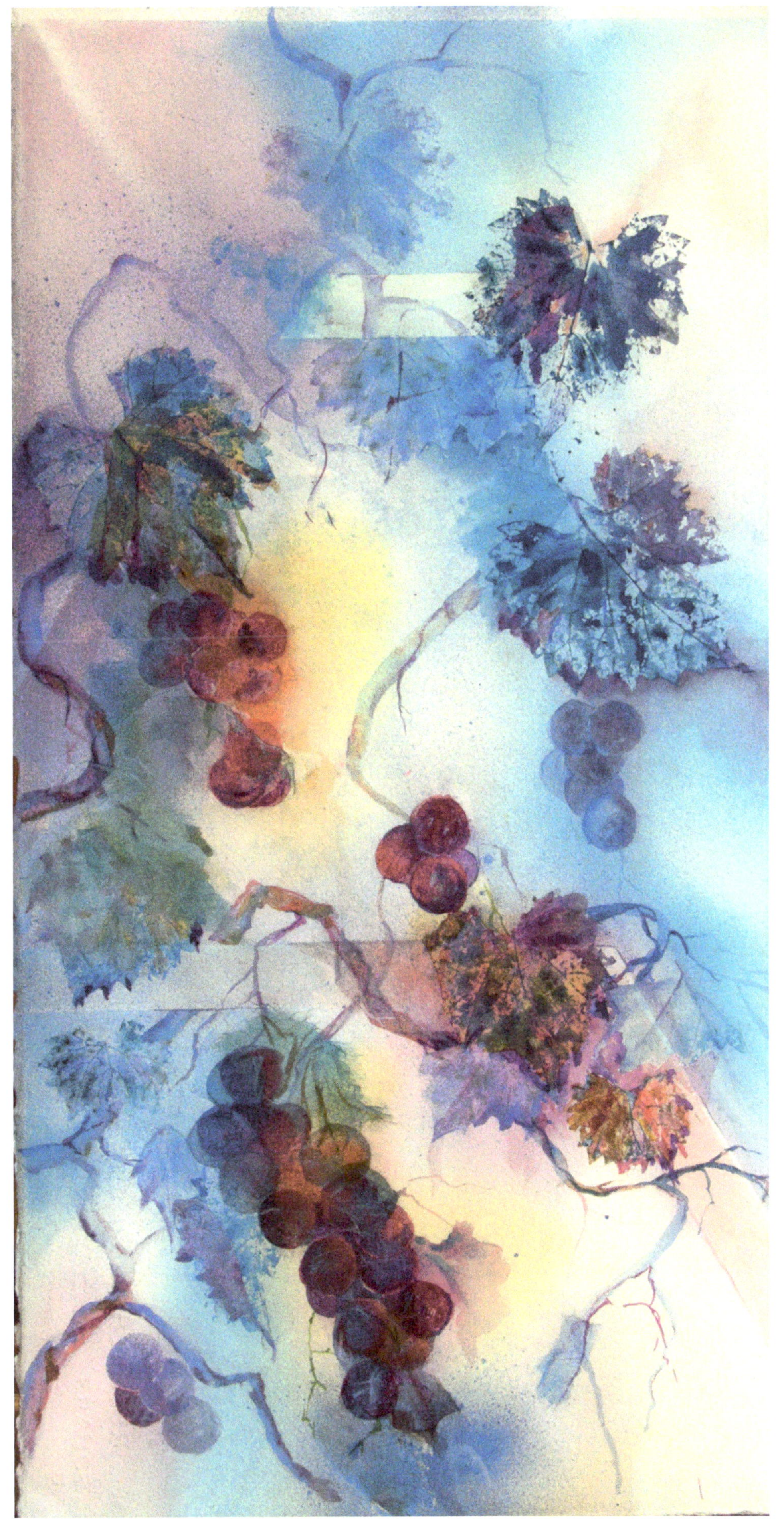

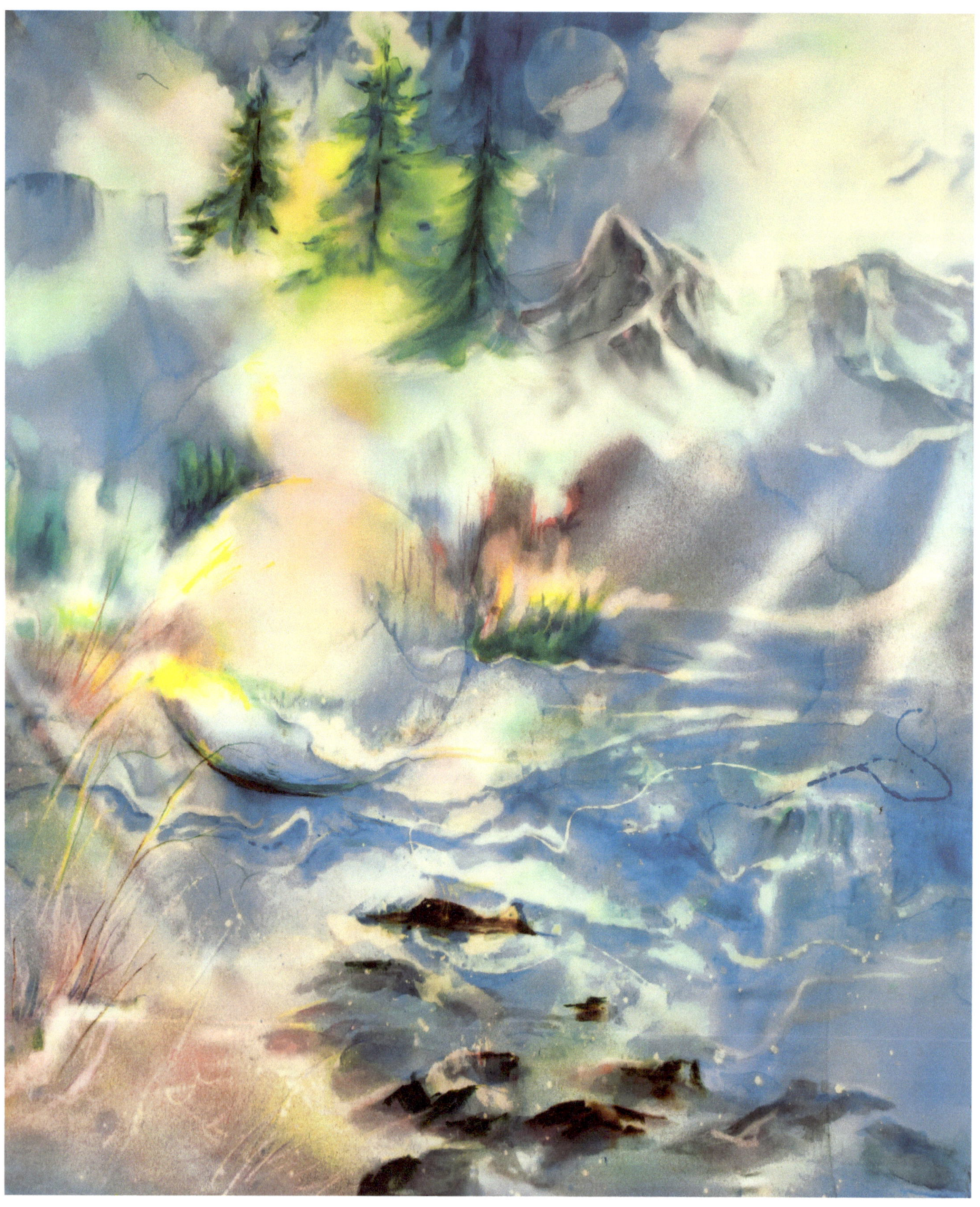

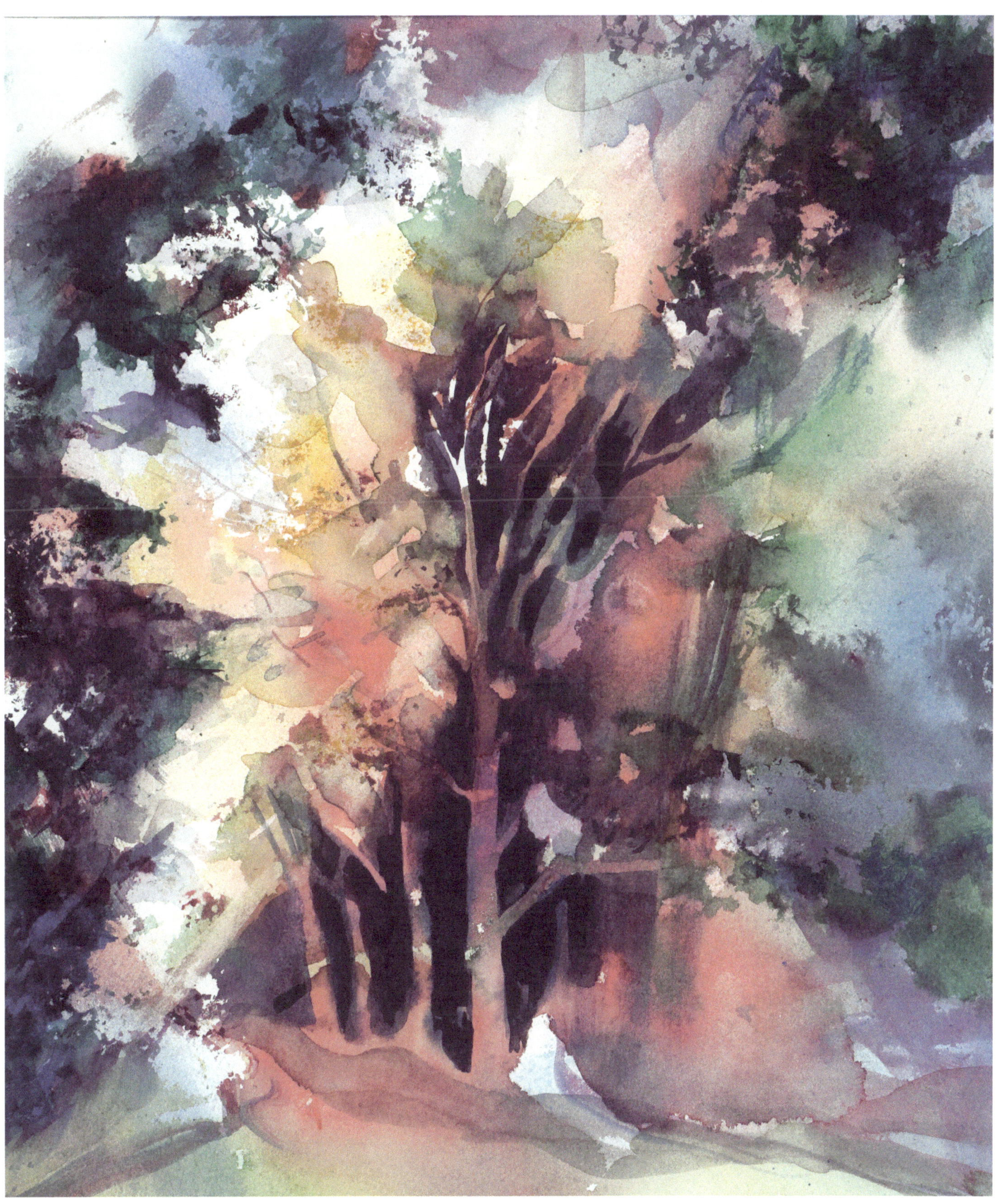

Summer

The heat has settled—
a hen laying its plump body on an egg.
Soon the air will be wet with thick summer fog,
hazy and burning white.
The lake grass moves,
carrying ghost whispers to the warm, brown ears of children.
Around me
  a squirrel stalking leftovers—
  the outrage of birds—
  the smell of still mud—

We dive, looking for that one cool, deep pocket.
We hold our breath, surrounded in a blanket of dim relief
Before bursting back to sun's drunk pounding.
What have we done on this summer day,
To deserve not the smallest breeze?
The body will shed its salty, salty tears—
the weeping neck, brow, eyelid—
and the furies of the mind turn to slow simmer.

Burial

You will see my round bones
in the gentle rain of leaves come Autumn,
robbed of flesh and powder-white, sanded to silt in
the rushing wind of winter and
rattling in dazzling maracas, shaking in
Spring.

I once held the blue crystals of snow,
my fists opening and there was nothing,
a cold whisper, the color of water.
Rising, by the cool taste of dawn,
Sinking by the moons drifting fingers.

Ten thousand years of bones underground,
a vertical layering of loss.
Each finger reaching to touch this song,
this same song.

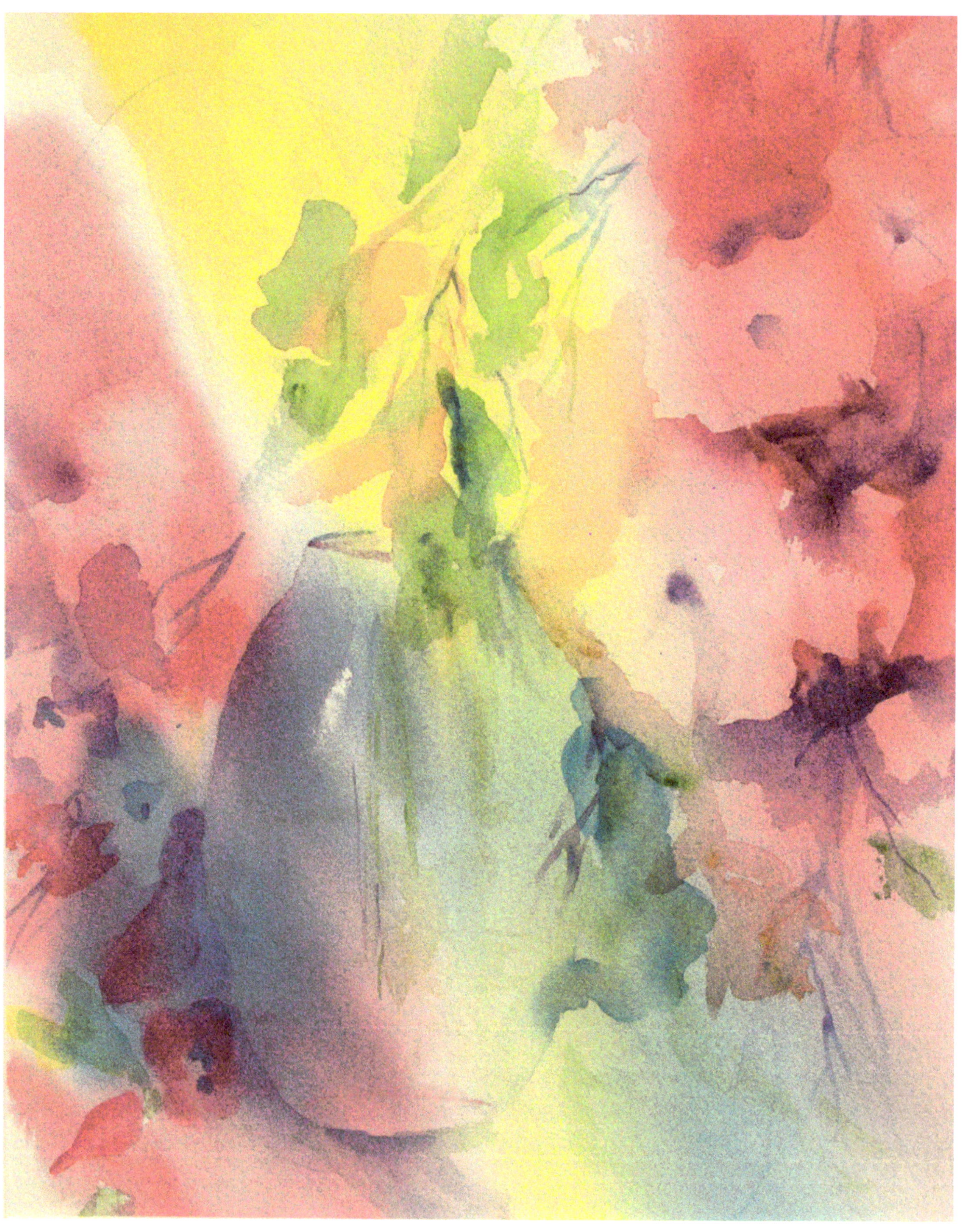

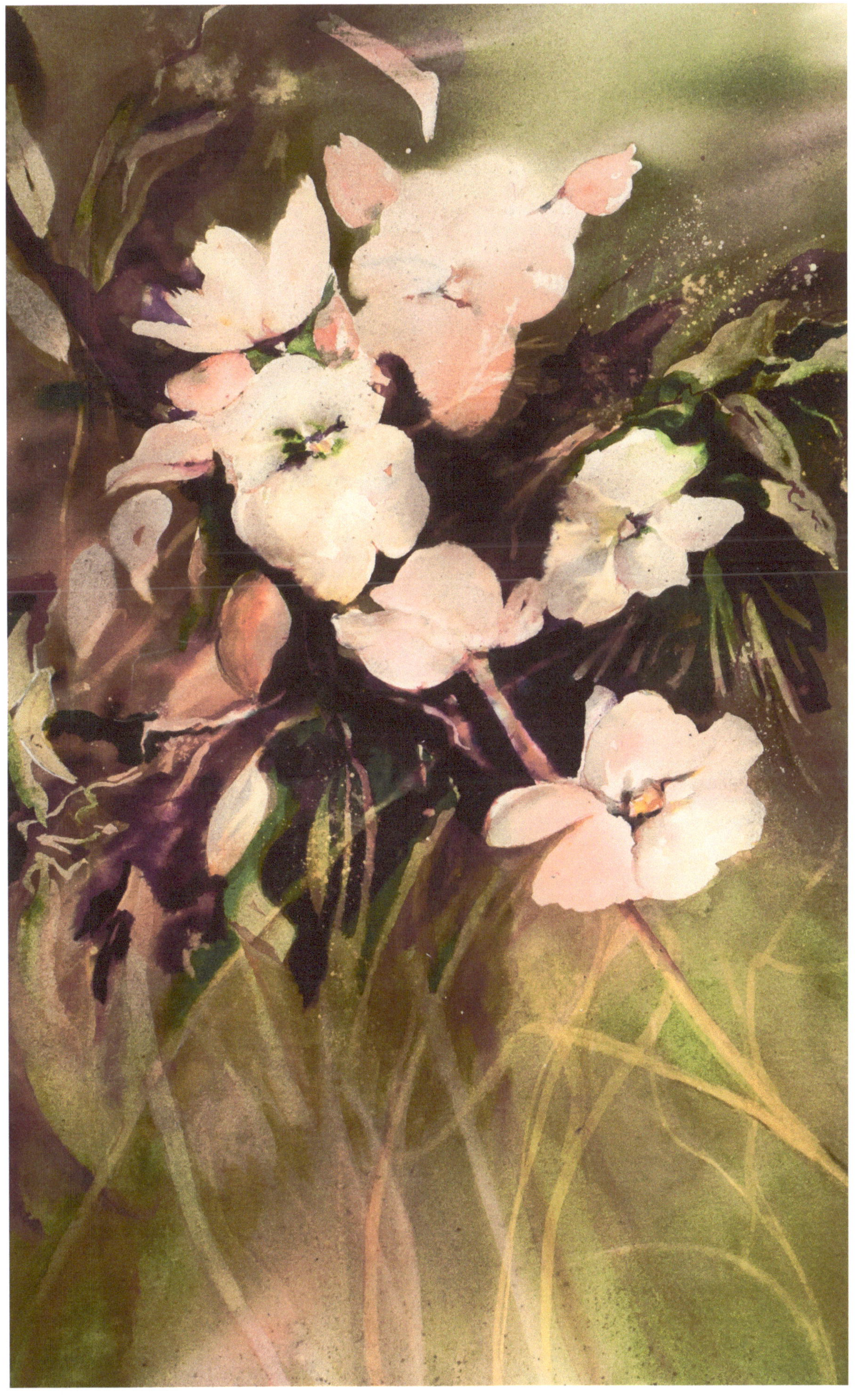

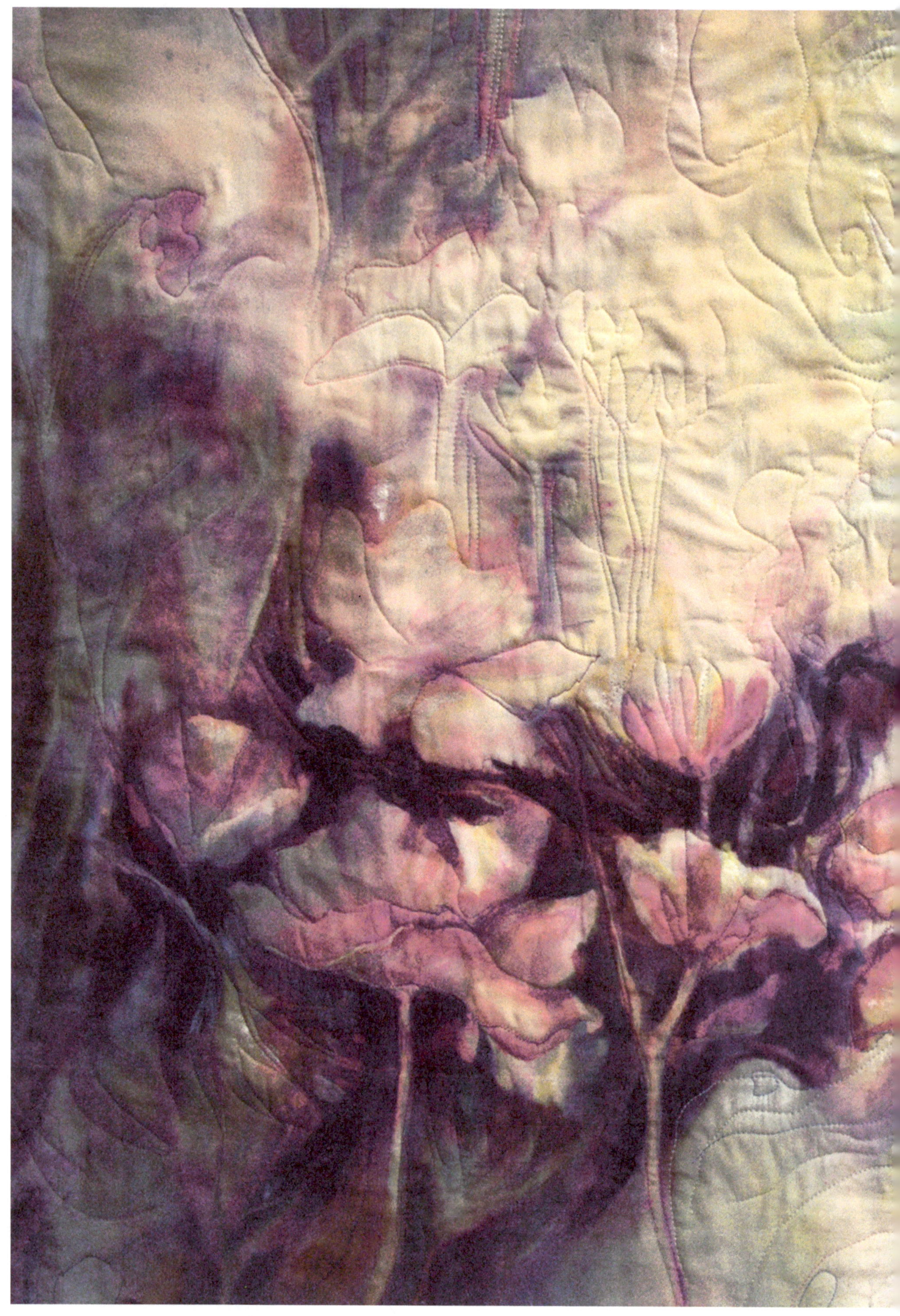

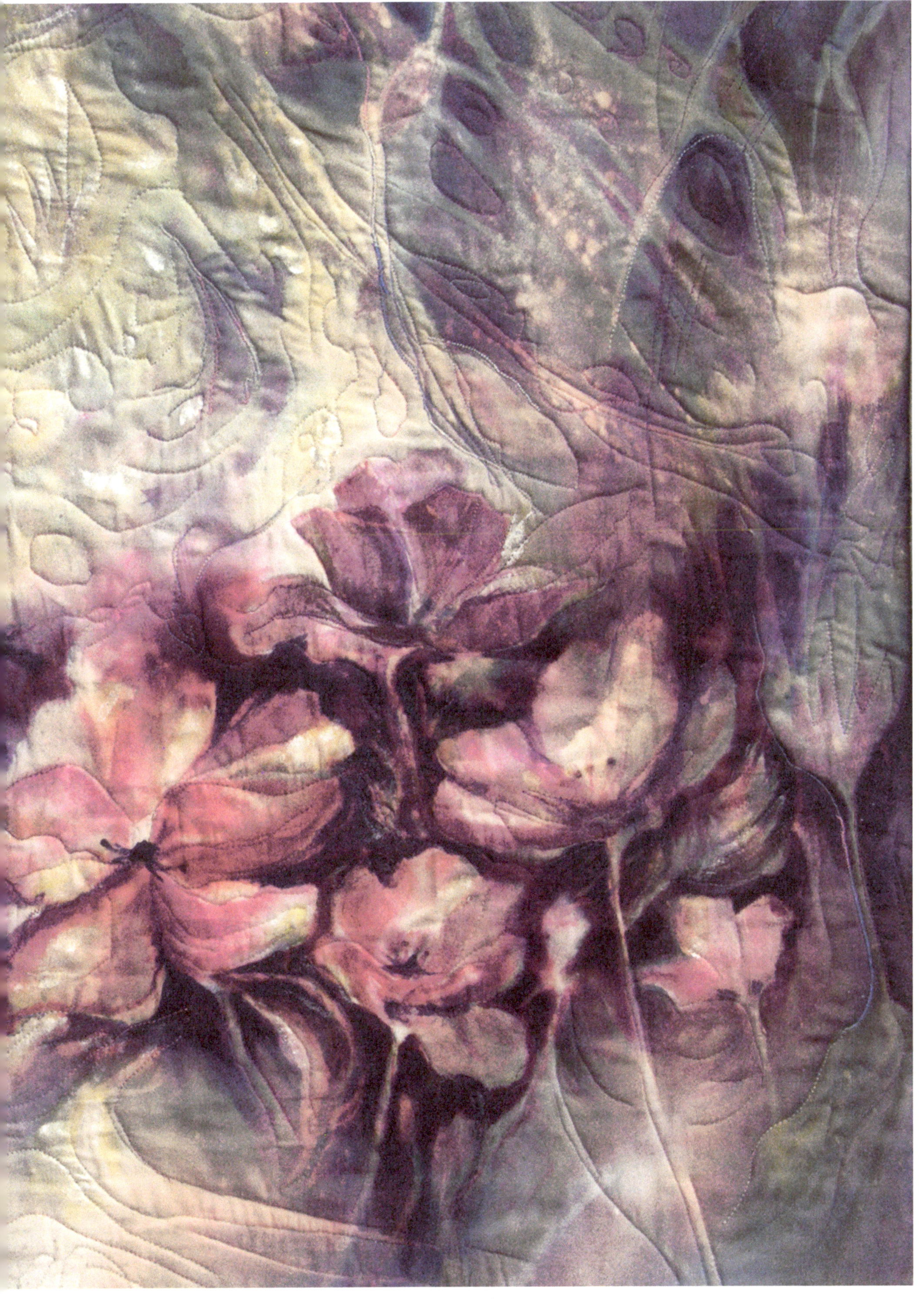

Footprints

There are marches across sandy stone,
my dear,
dusty feet that grind out prints,
round scoop of toes,
deep curve of the heel bone.

We carve our true way in the sand,
tip-toeing or pounding
the new bi-ped way,
leave behind a history,
a trail of smoke.

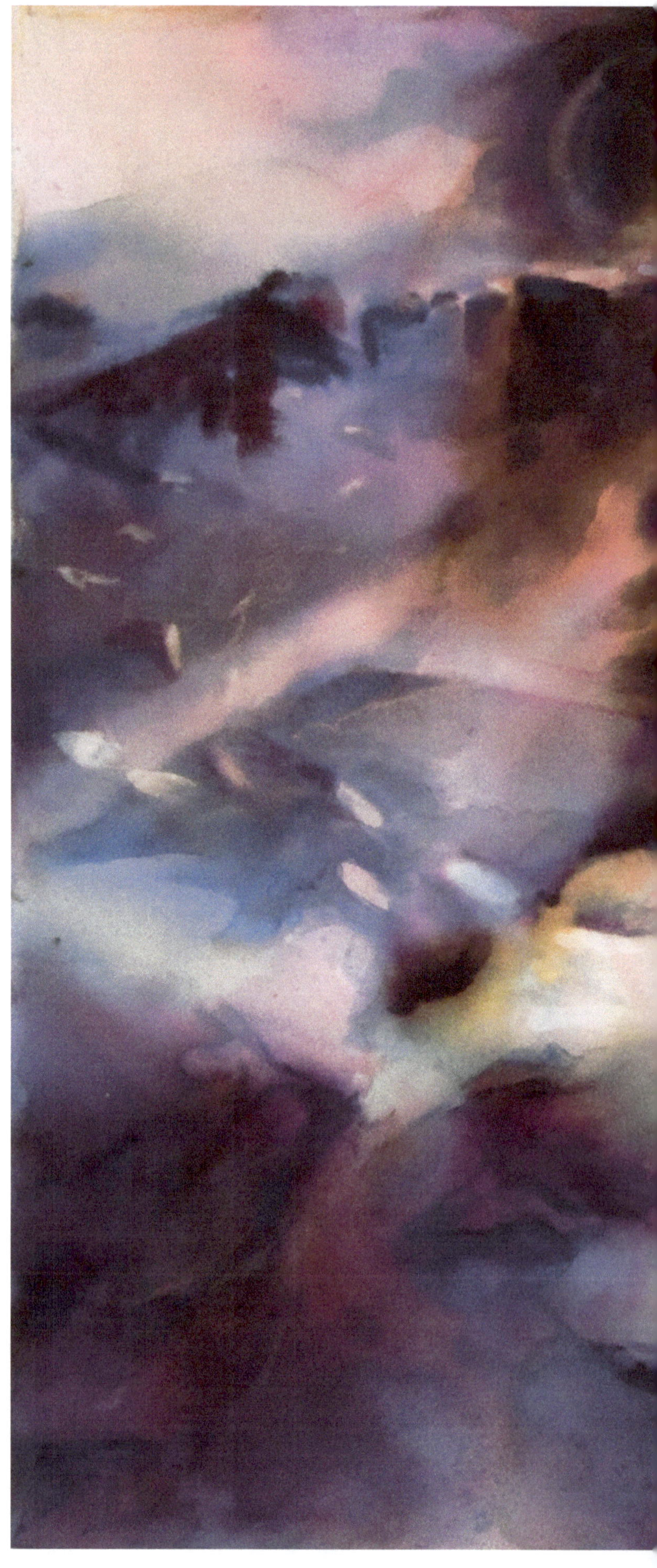

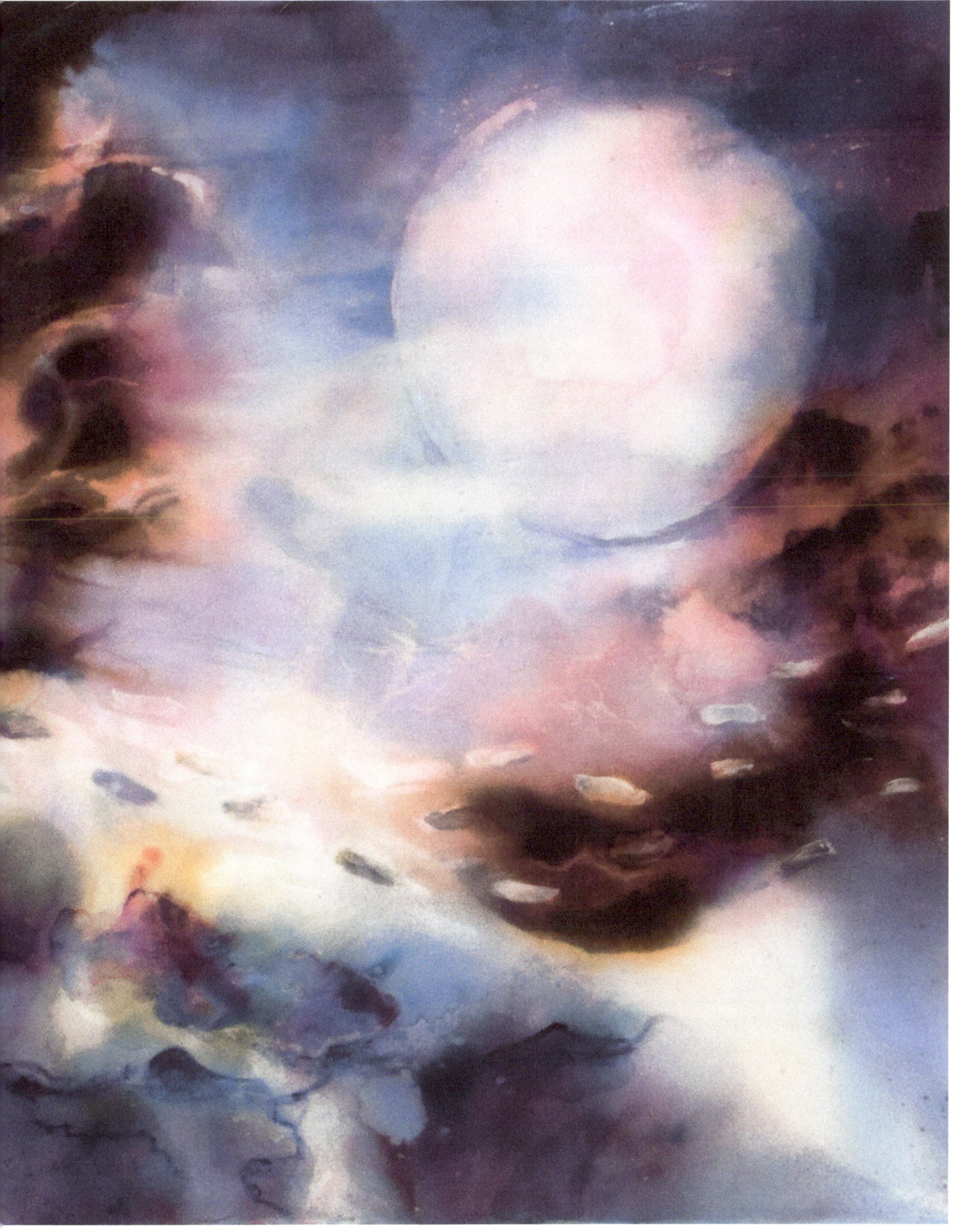

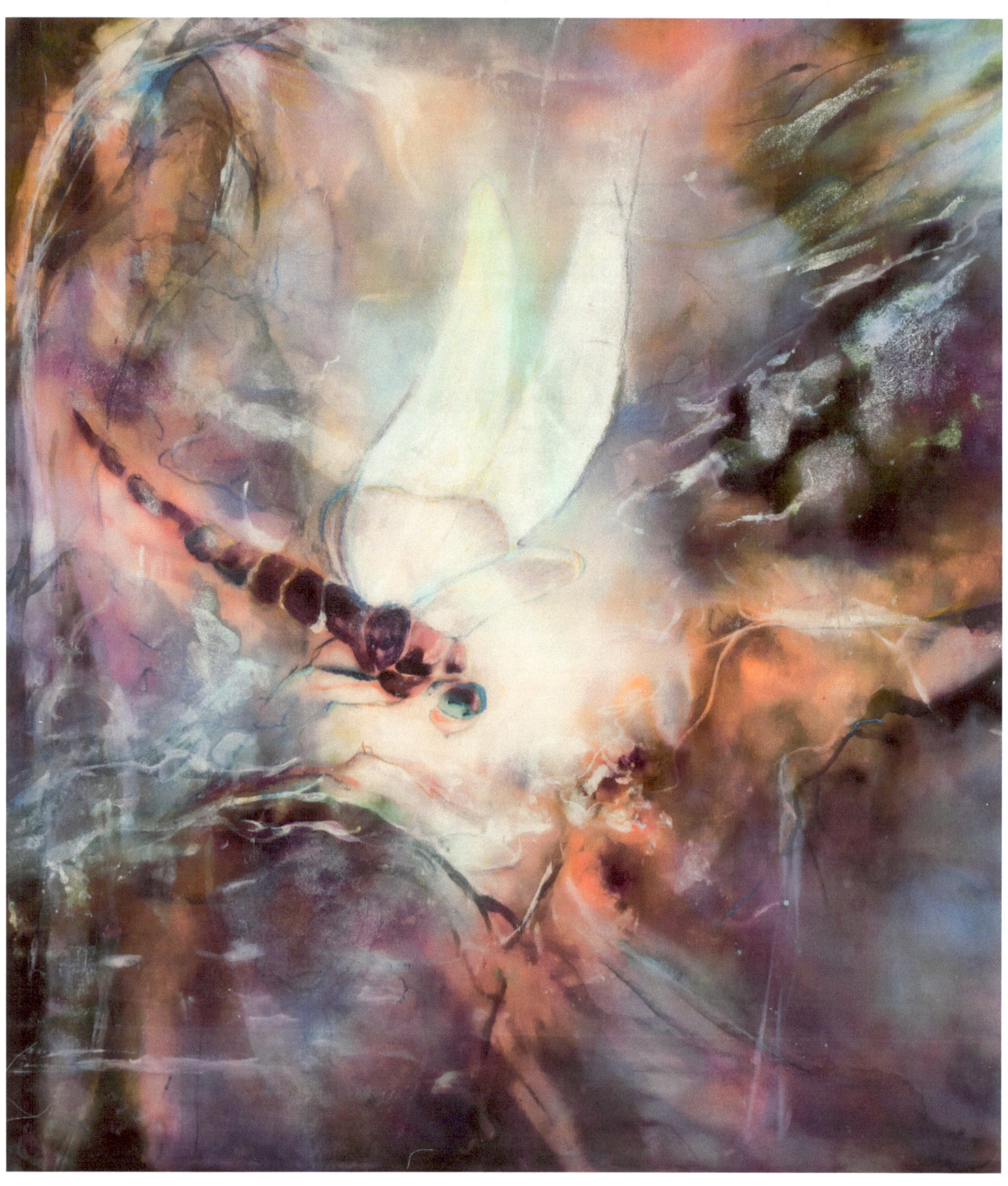

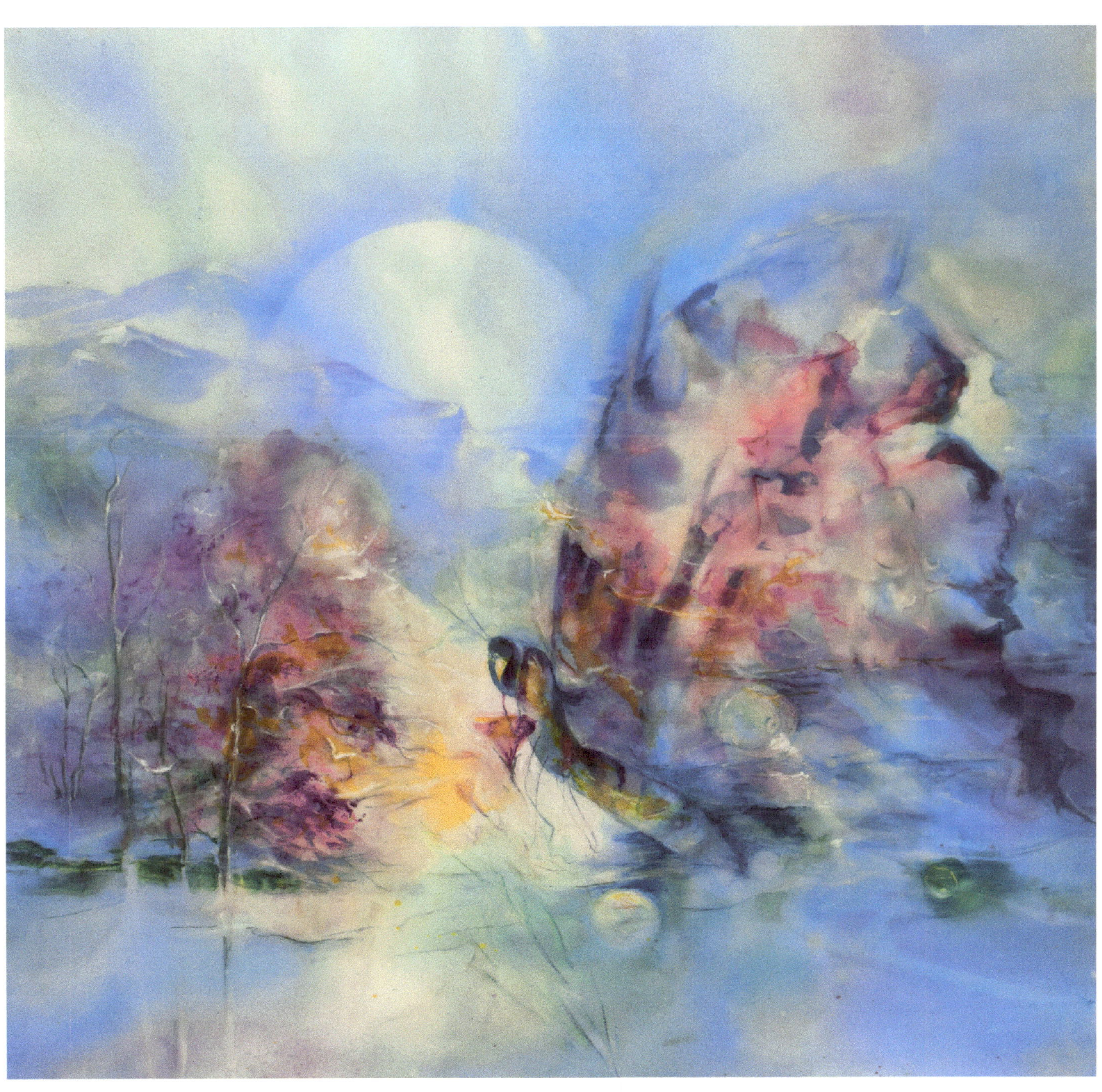

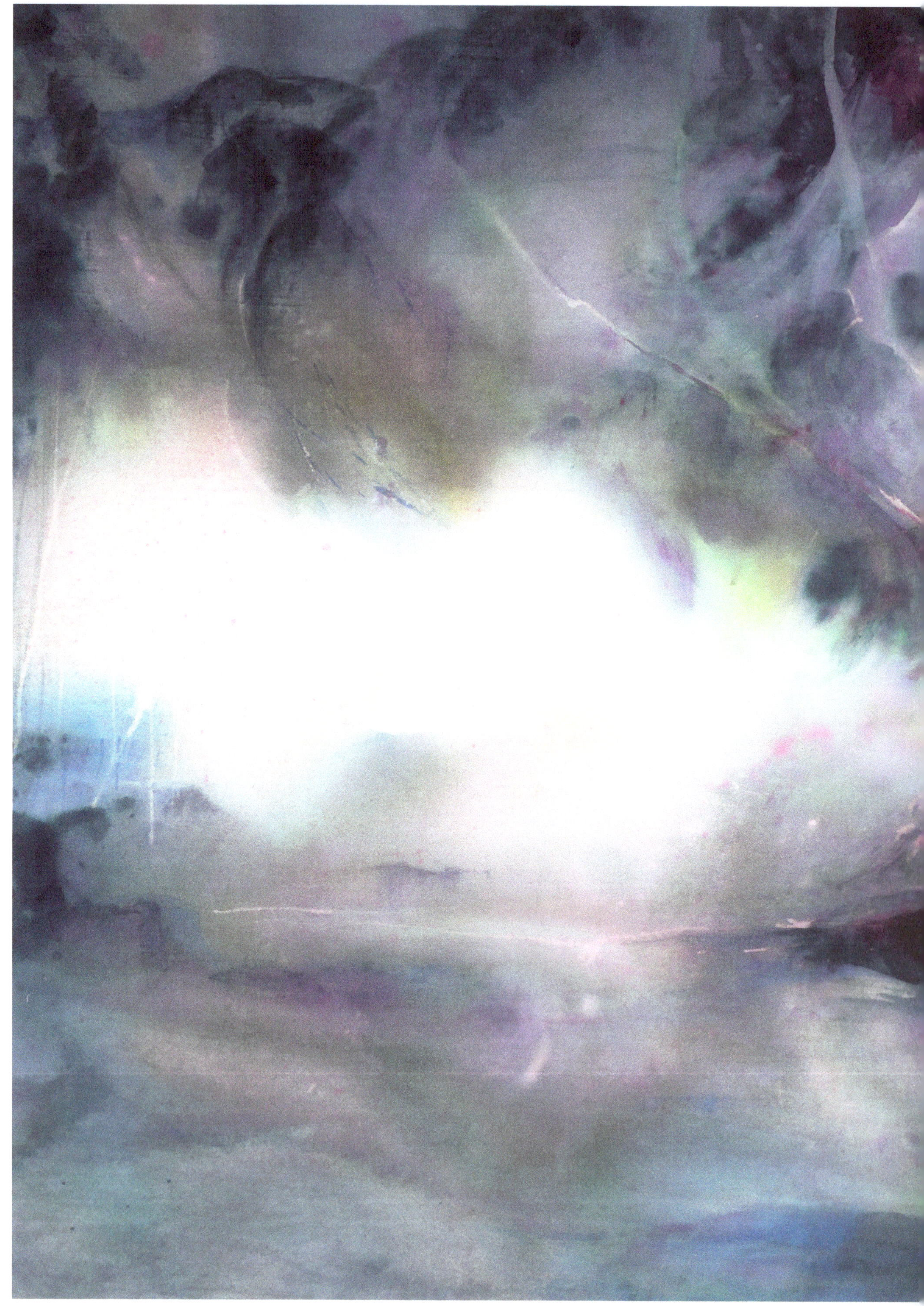

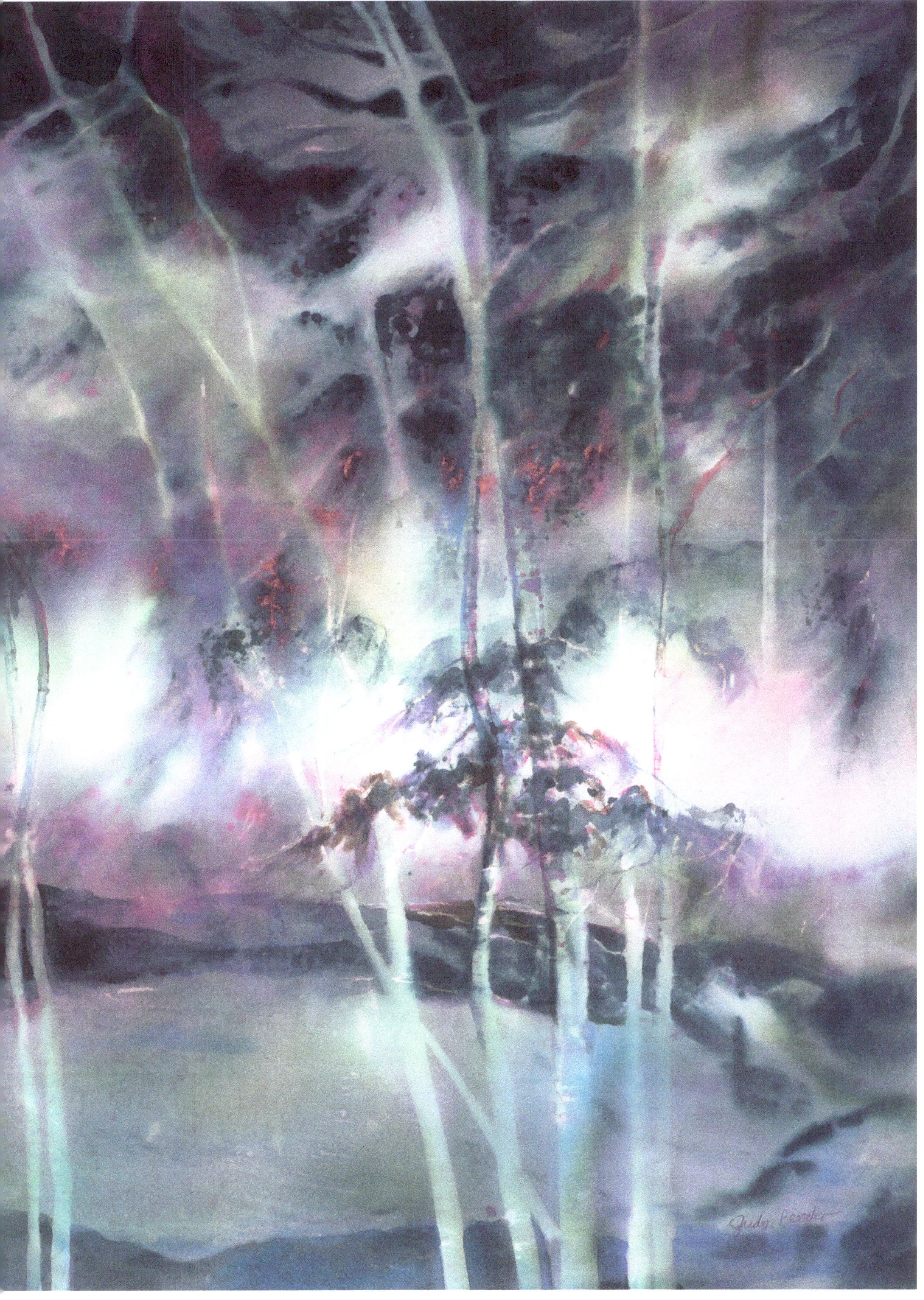

Sand and Glaciers

Long birds stretch shadows
like ghosts on the ground,
a secret evening flight.

Time moves shifting sands,
a billion winds that soothe longing
into slow, round dunes.

One day we will slip under.
We are gone, and here, and gone.
Whispers.
Drifts.

Somewhere a silent glacier
grinds an icy path,
Colossal,
Blue.

Somewhere in that silence
is a memory of you.

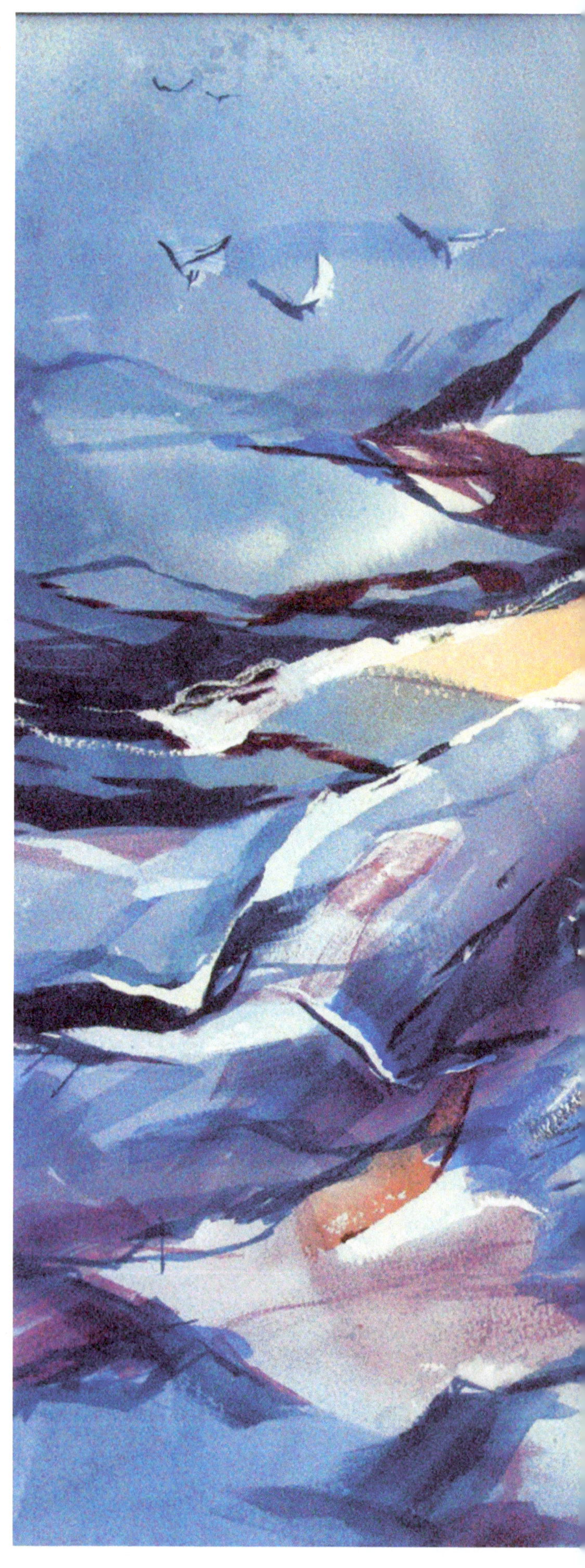

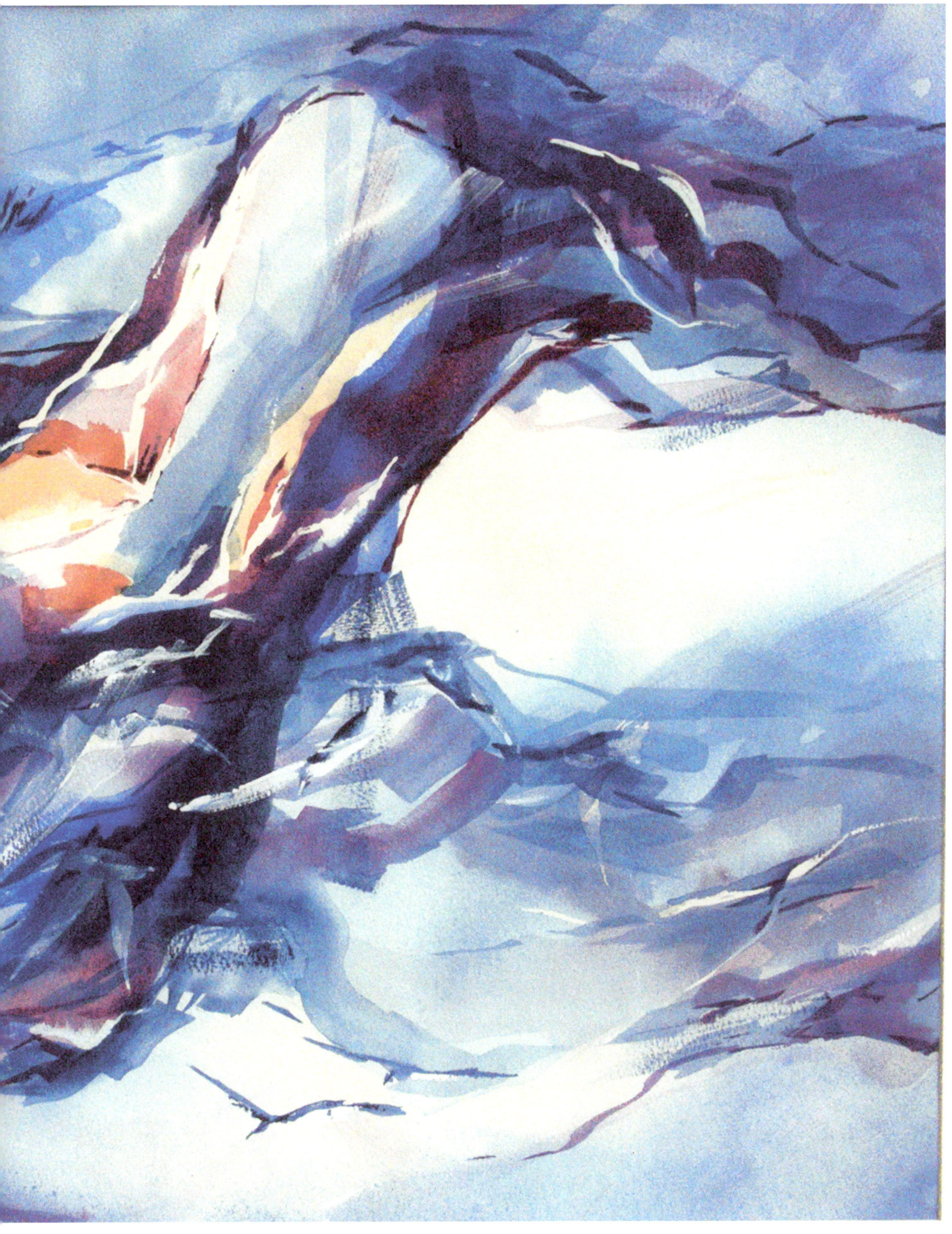

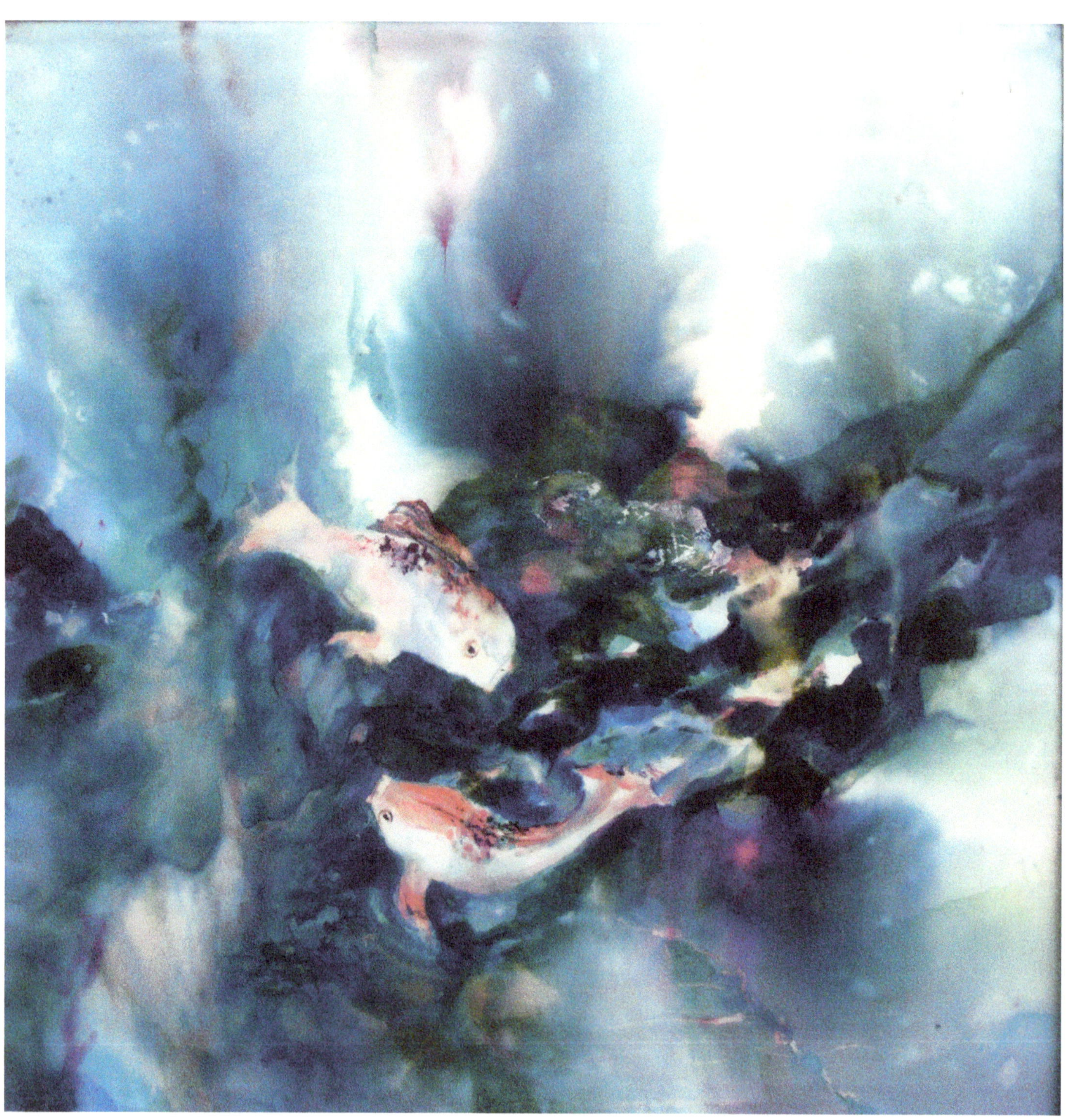

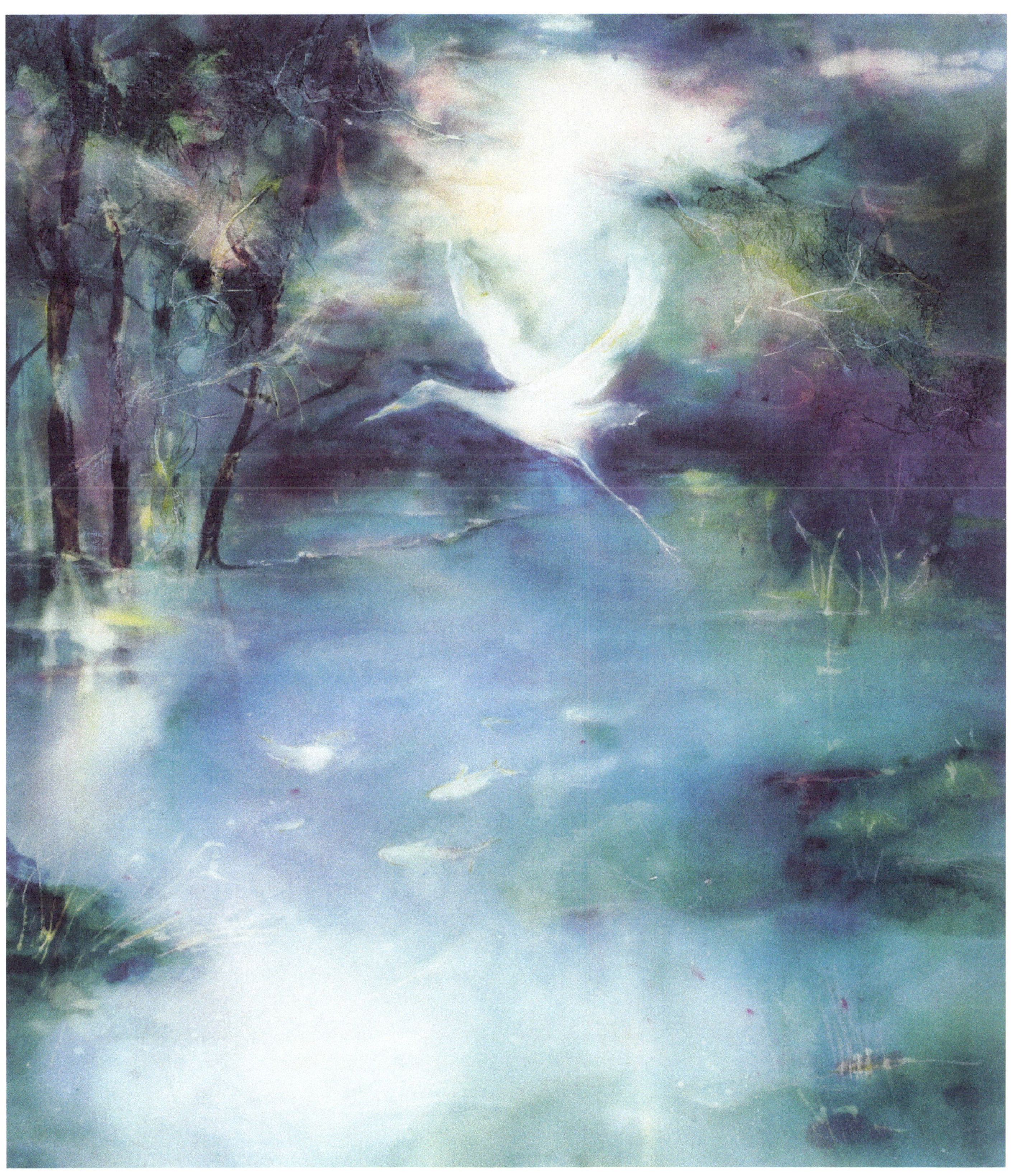

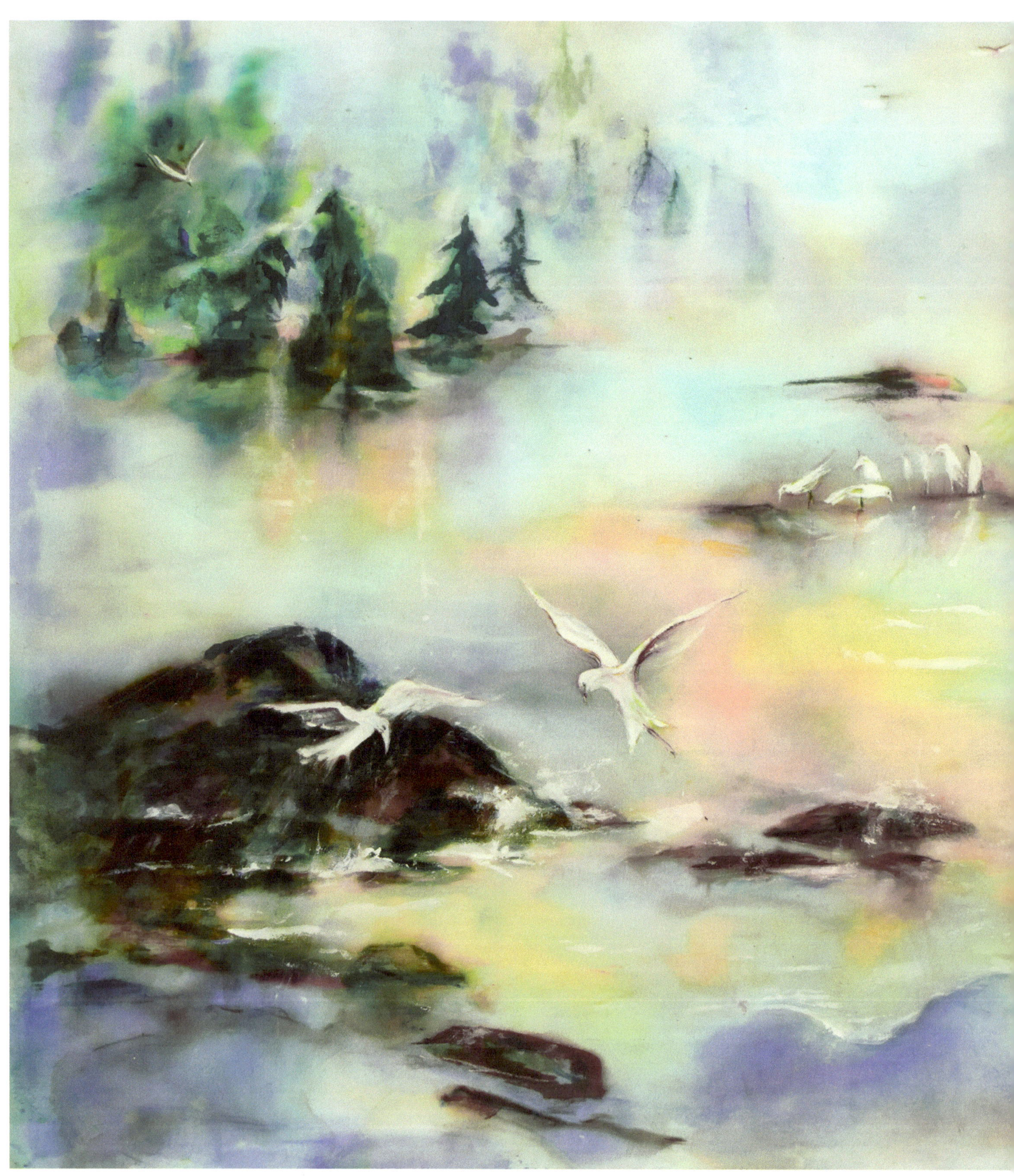

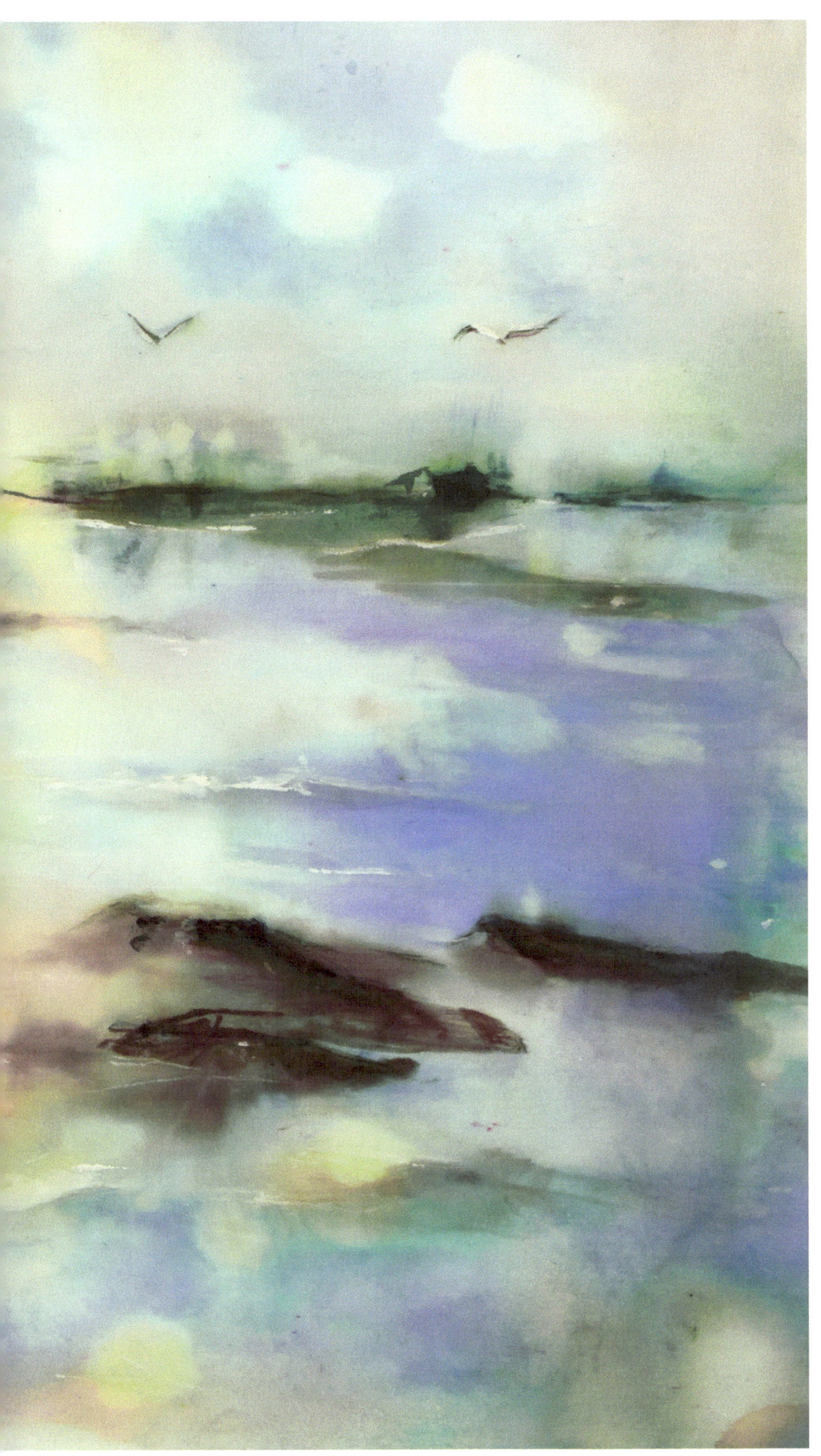

Storm

The sea has labored,
It's argument made again,
pounded on the shore.

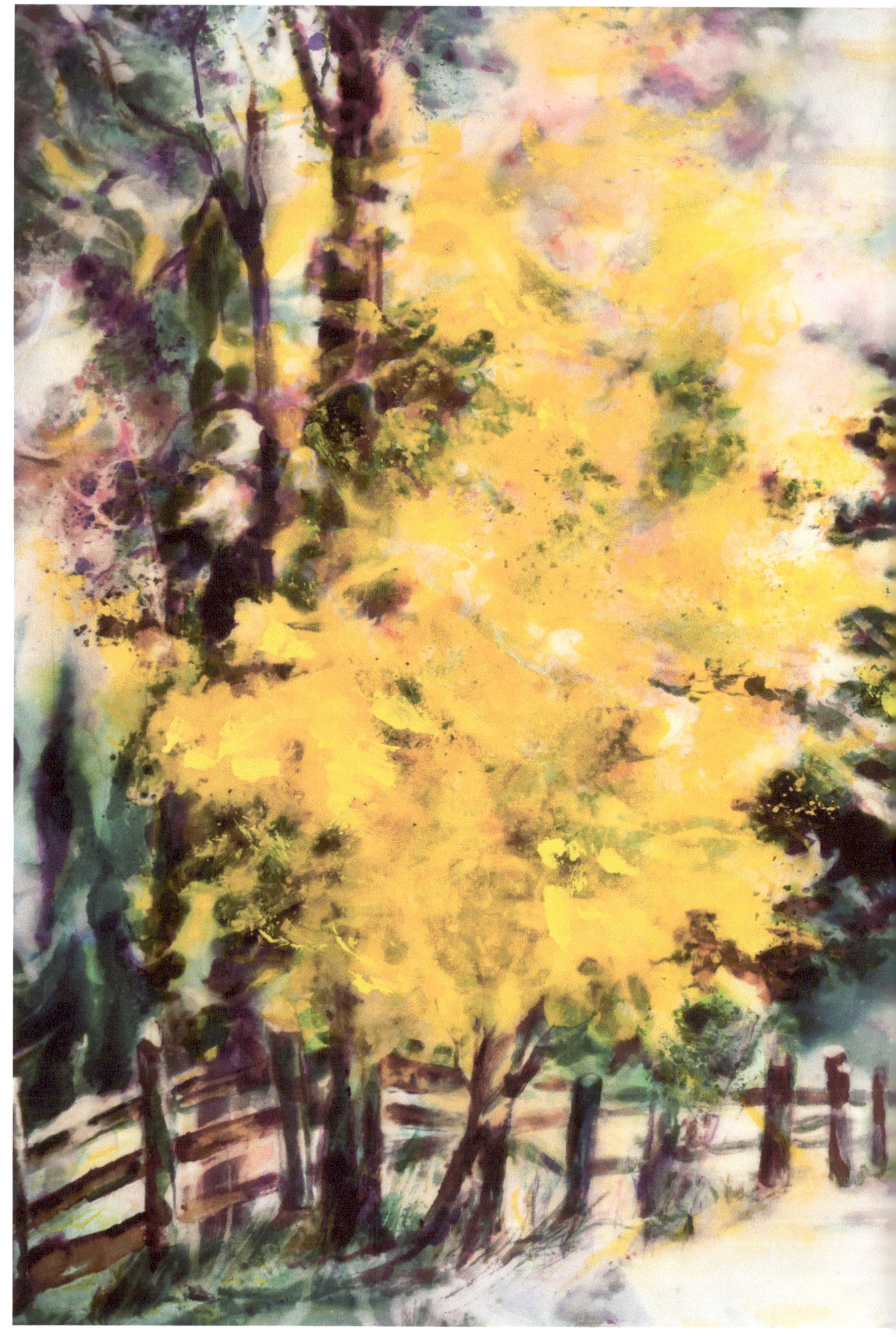

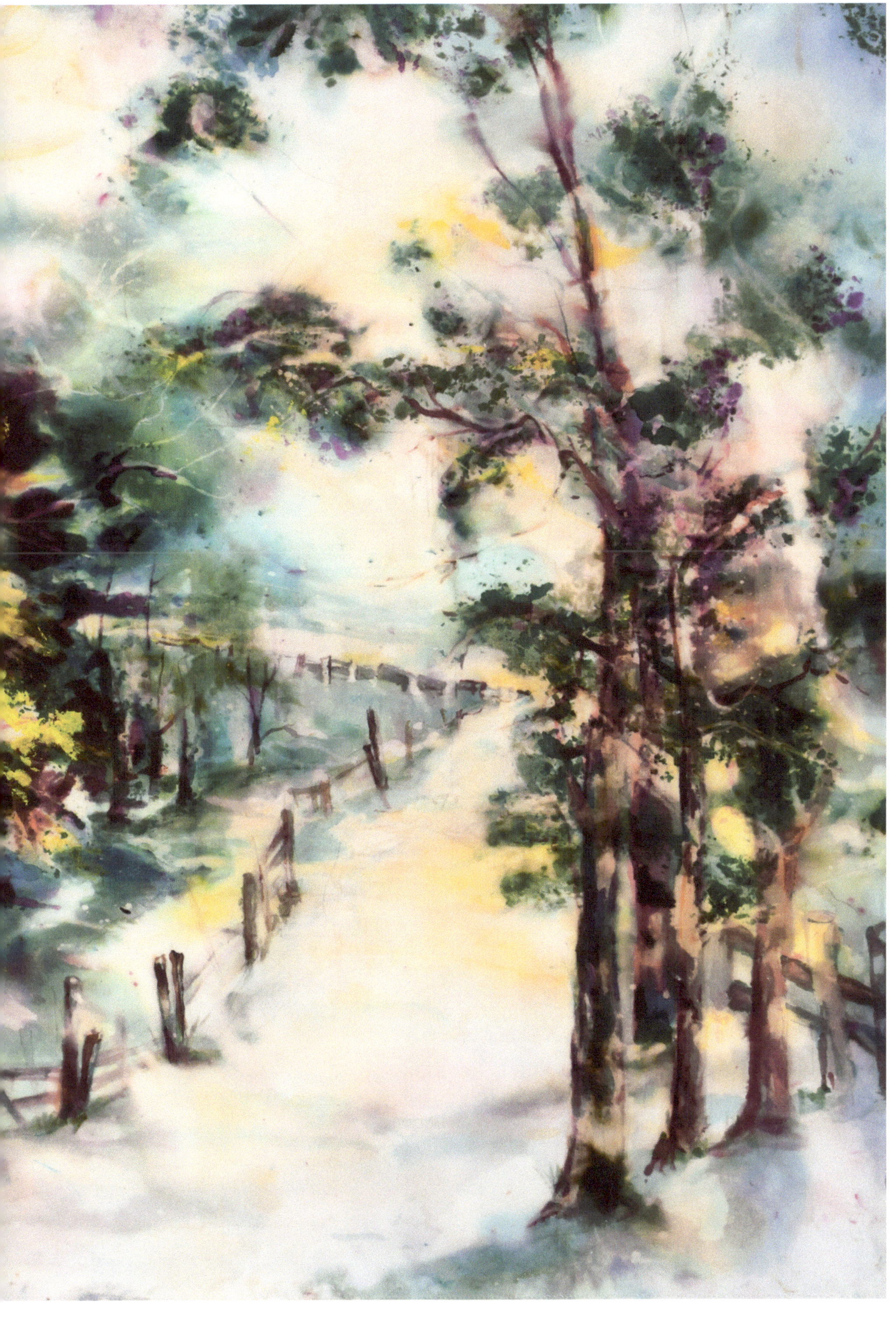

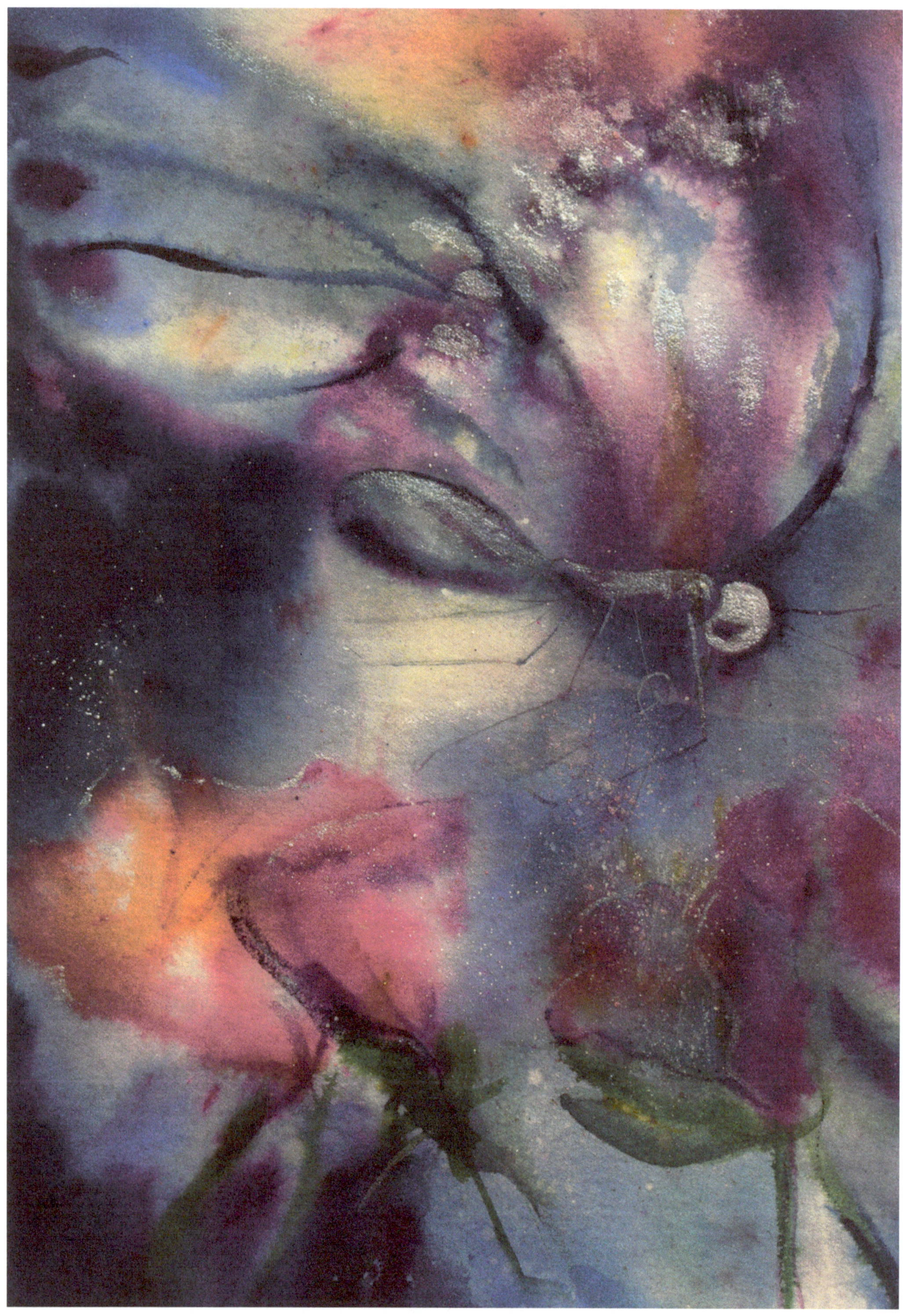

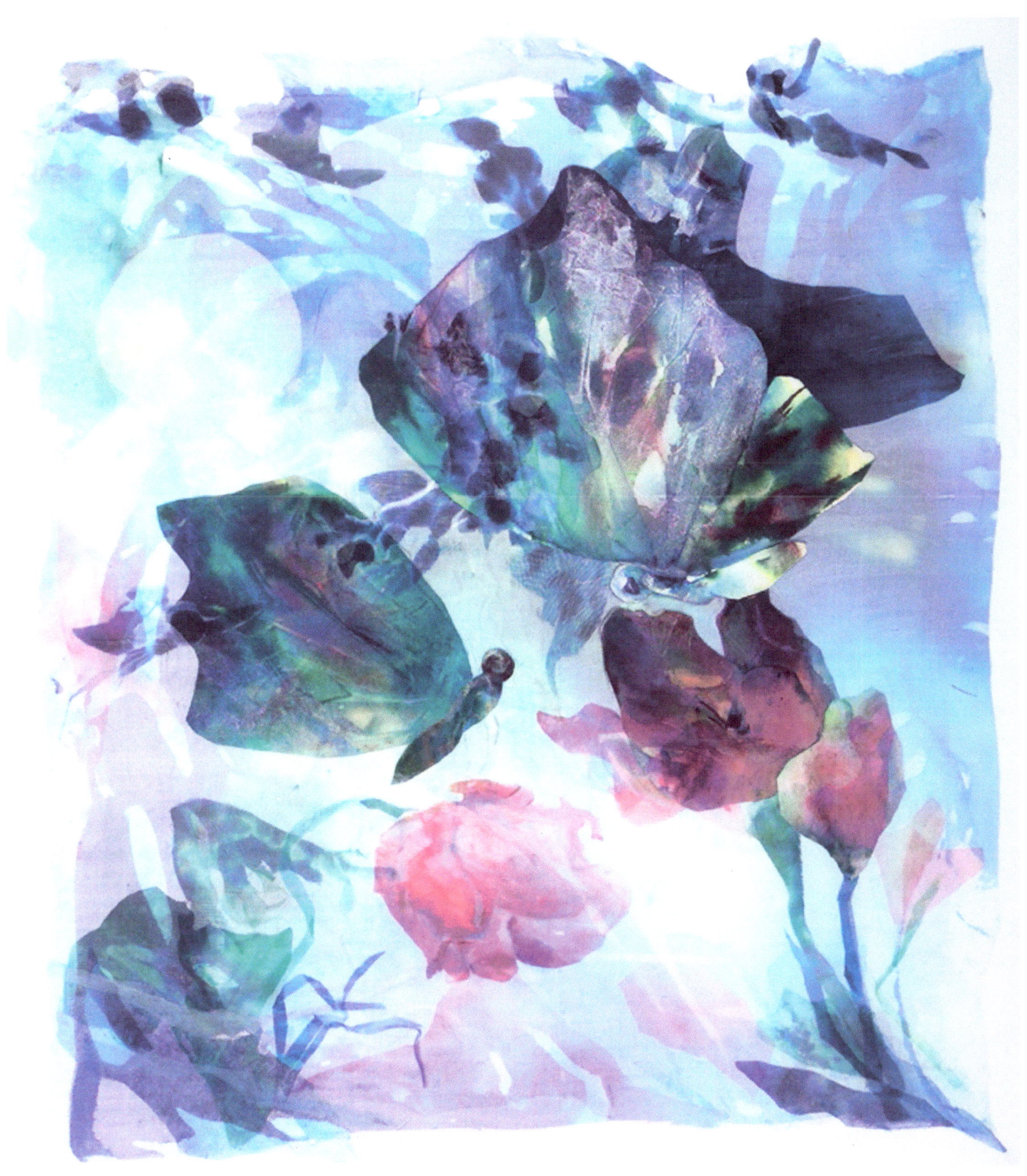

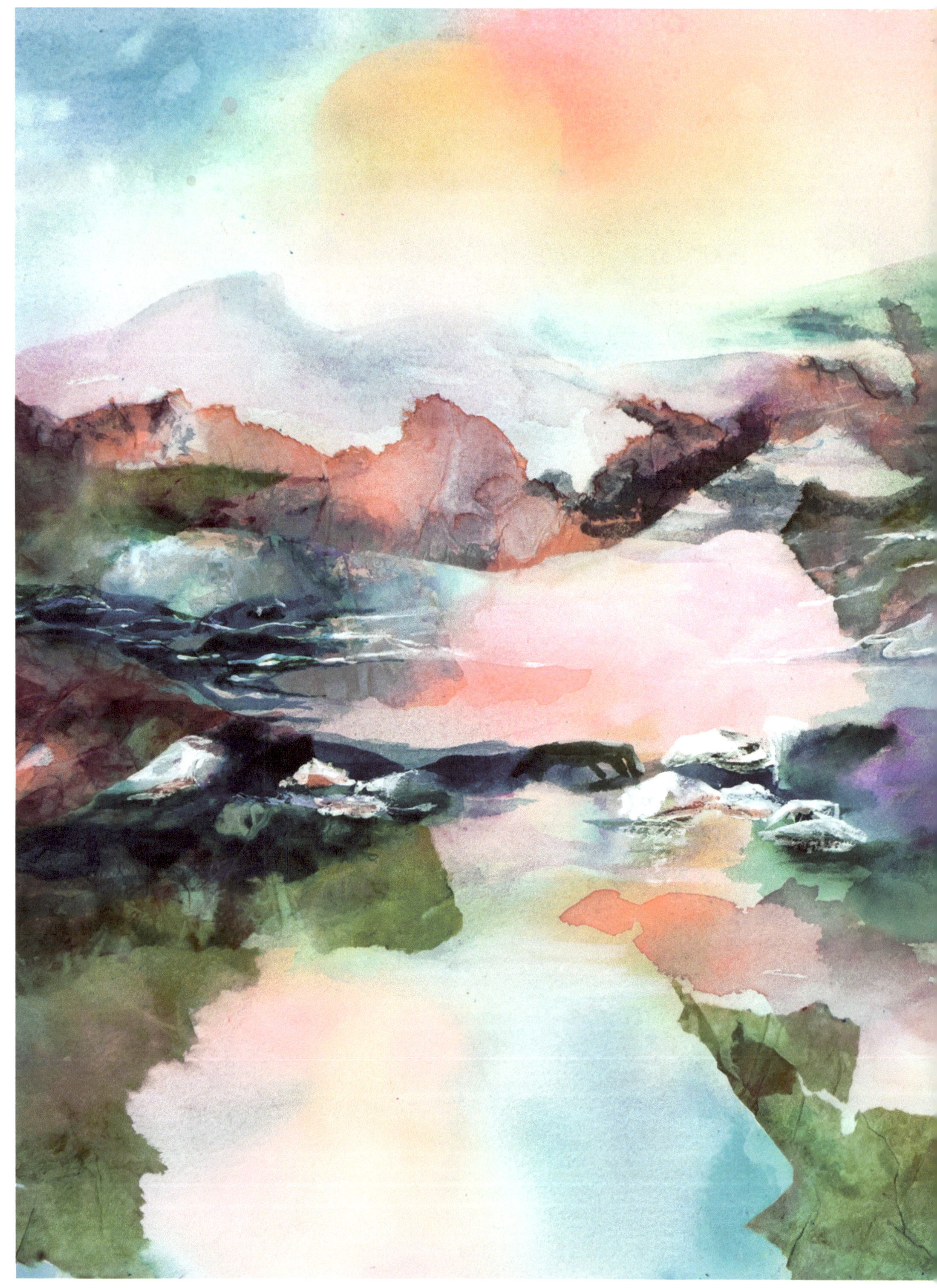

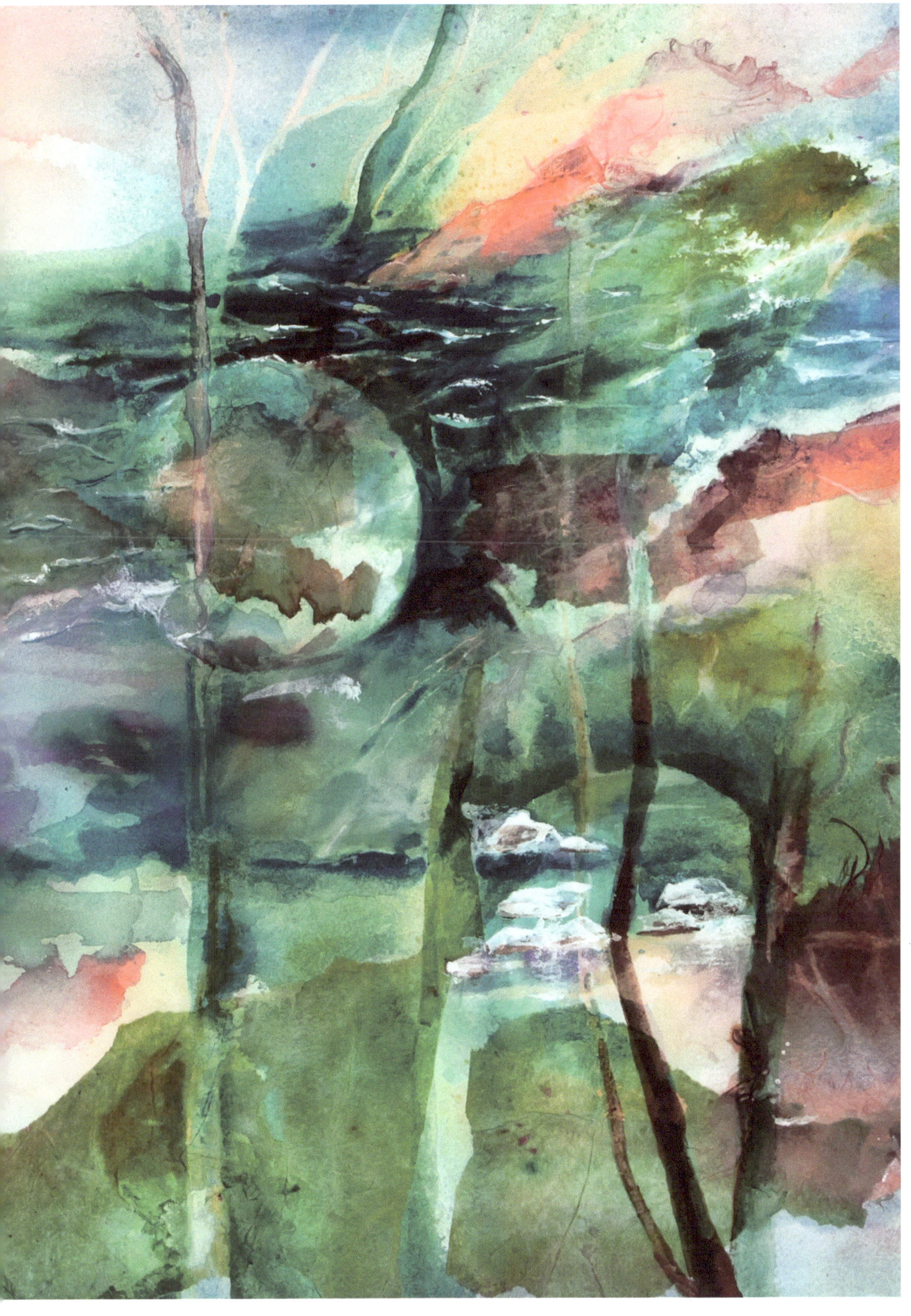

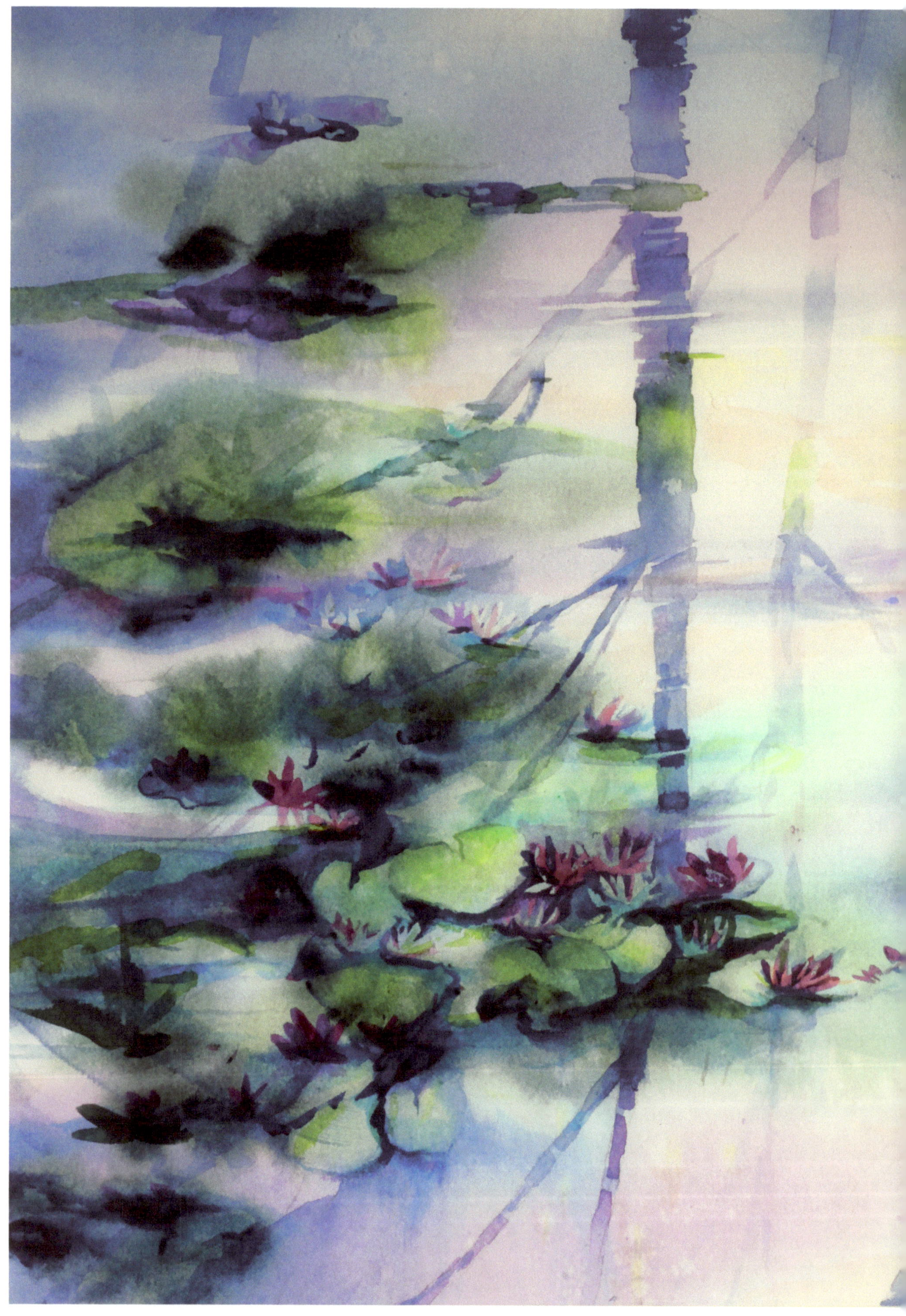

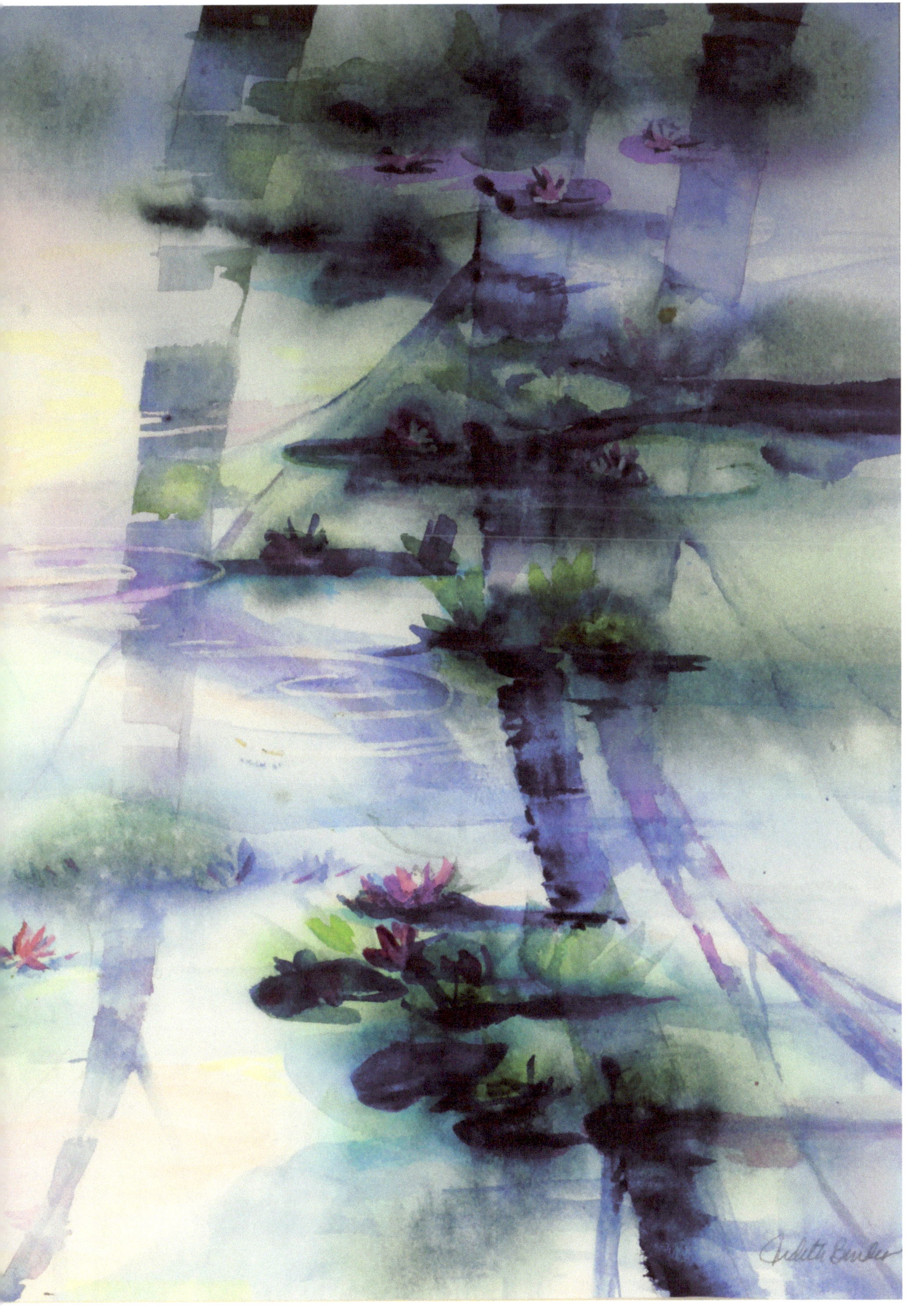

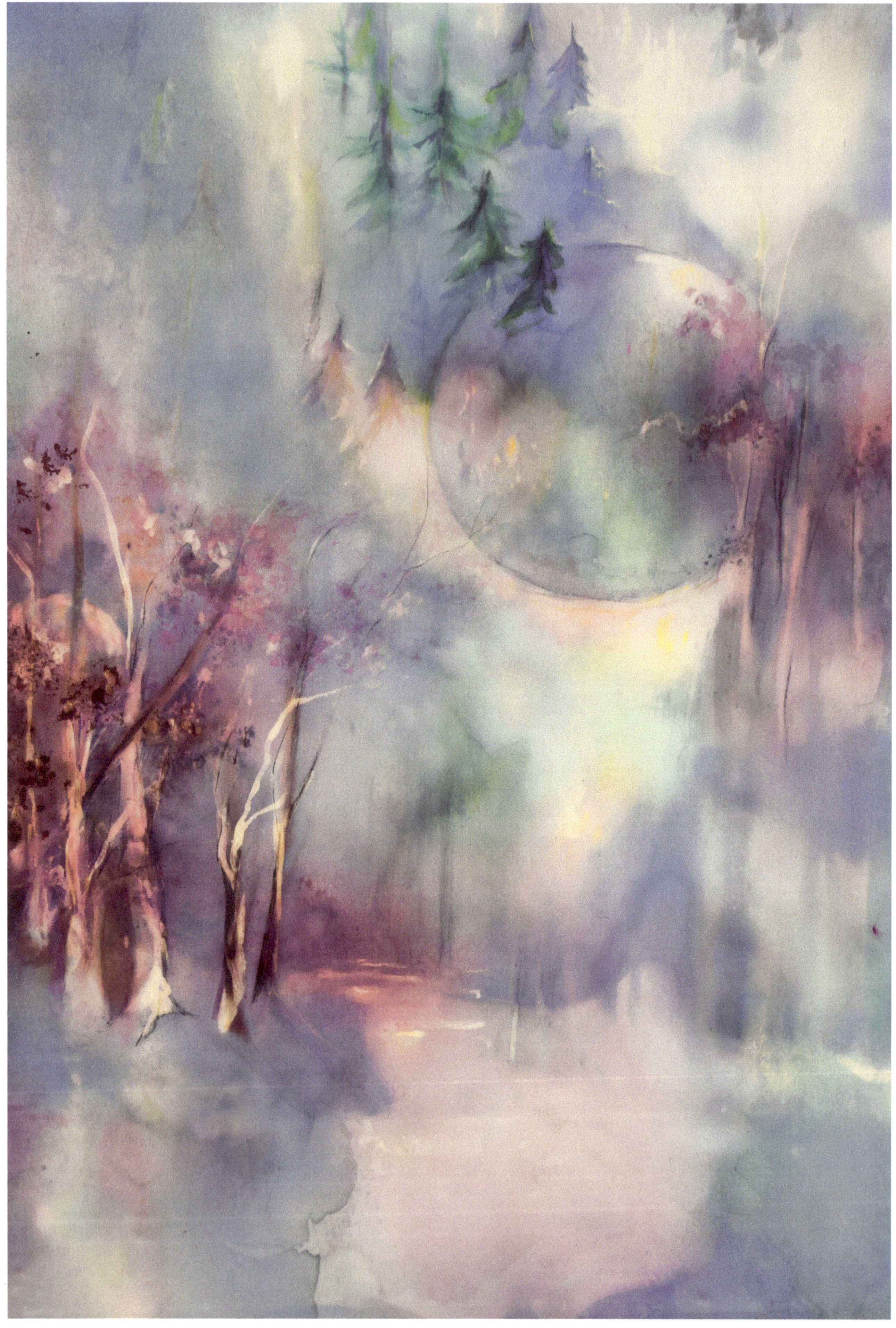

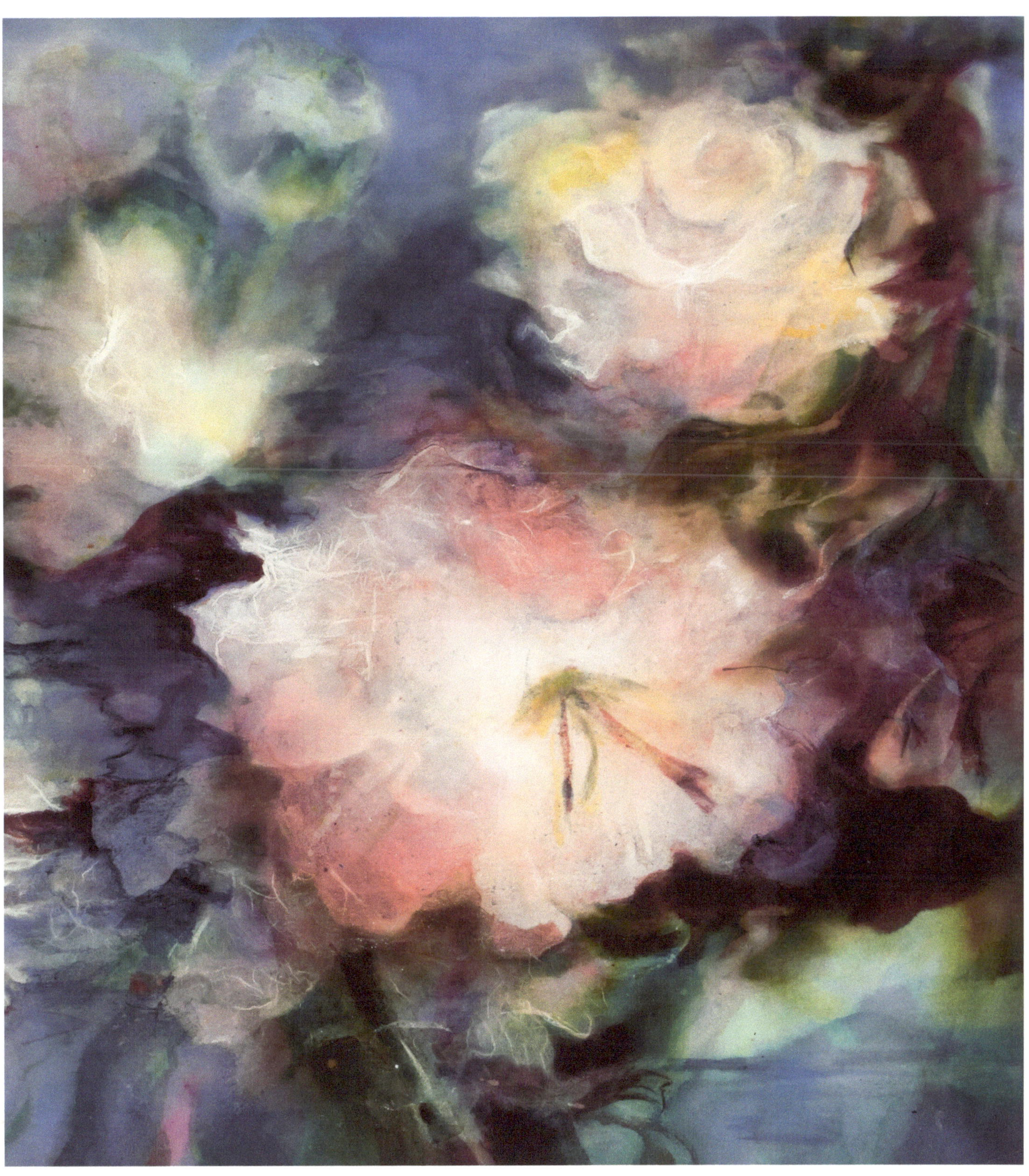

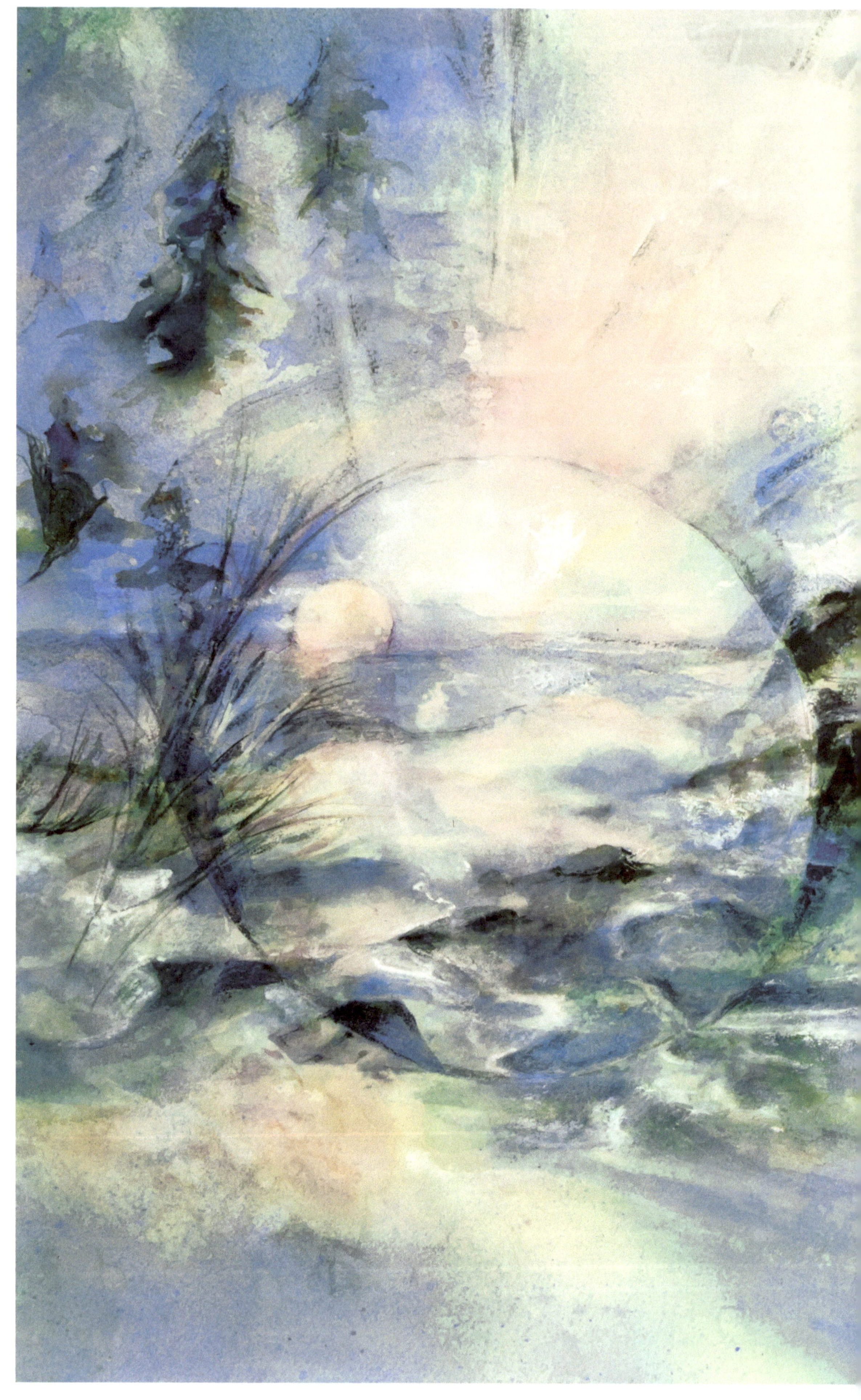

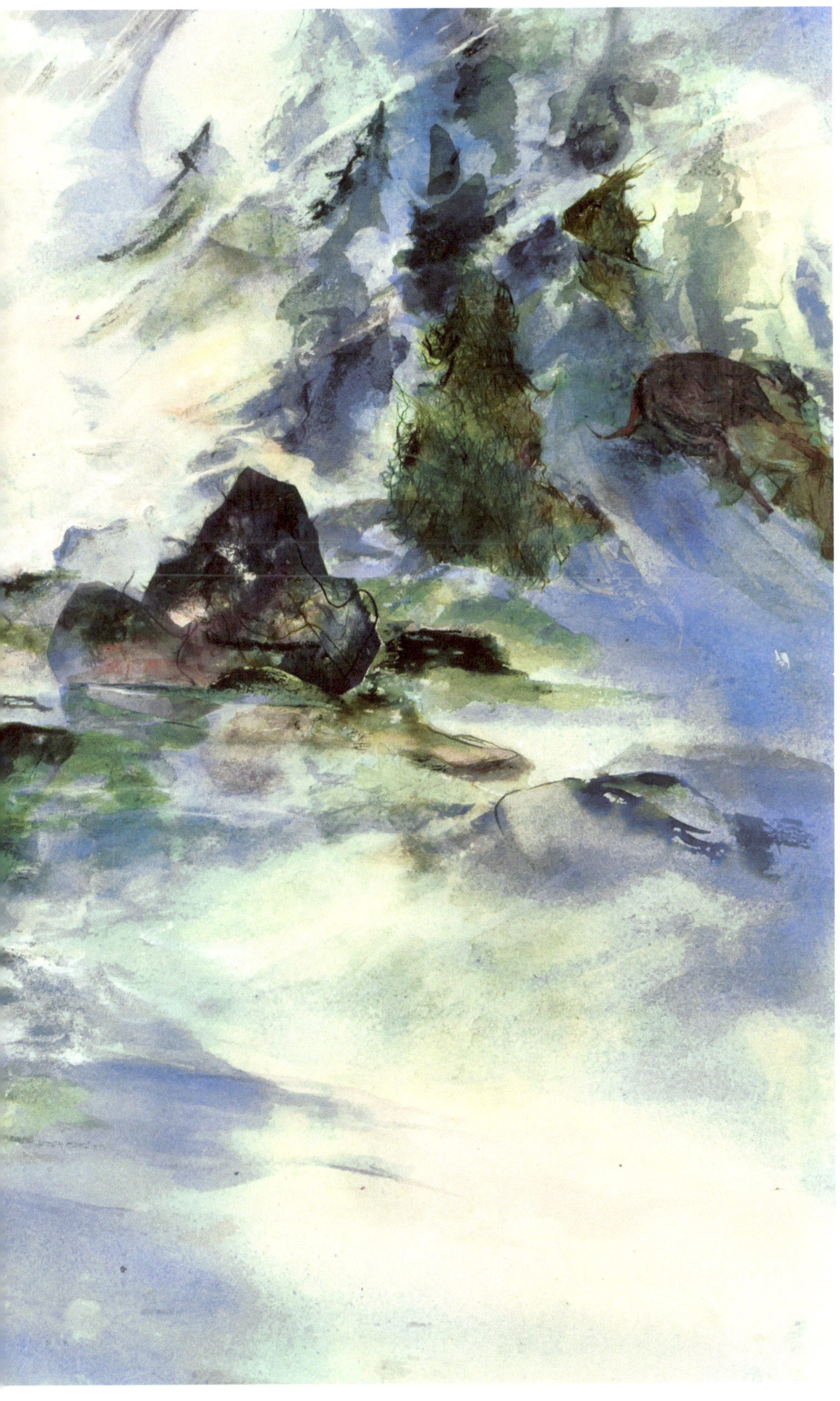

Fog swells,
drifts and settles
in cool, misty clumps
in the dark
on the road

I am walking and not thinking.
My face is damp and my lips are wet.
My eyes are red from cold breezes.
I am older, and uncertain.

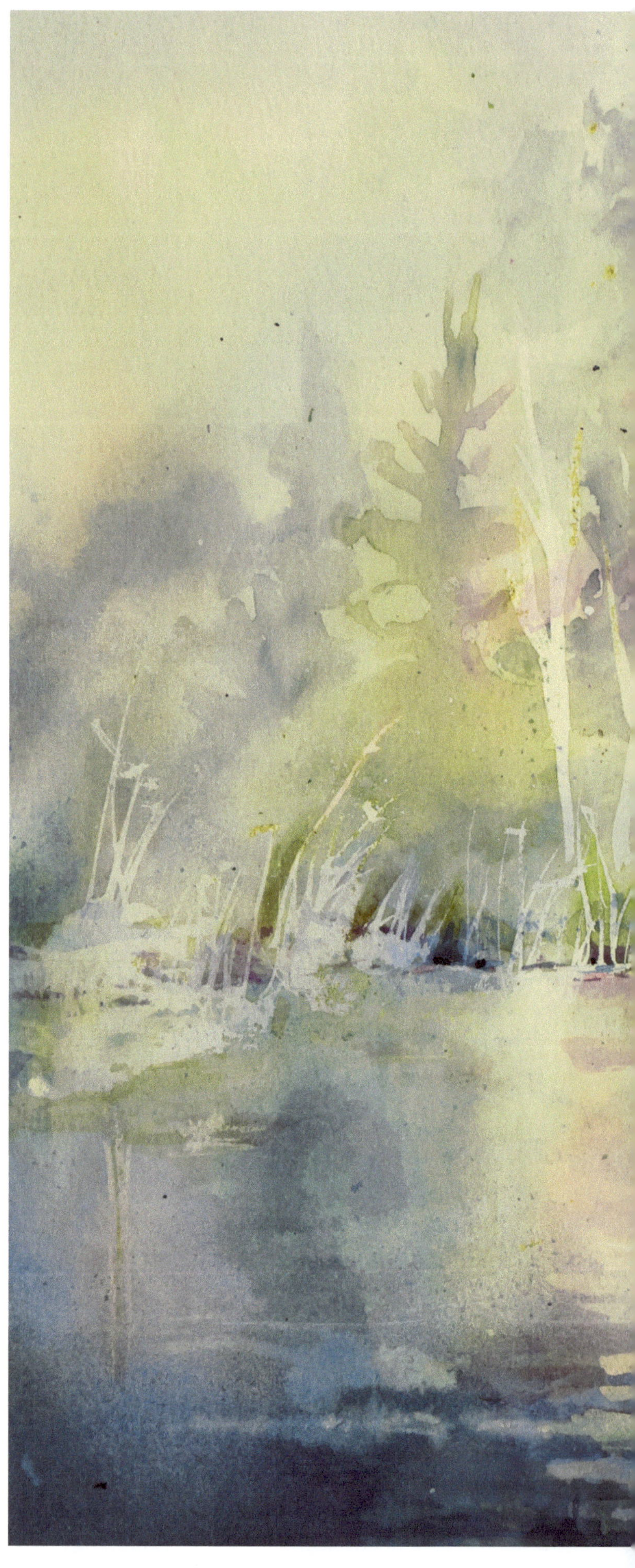

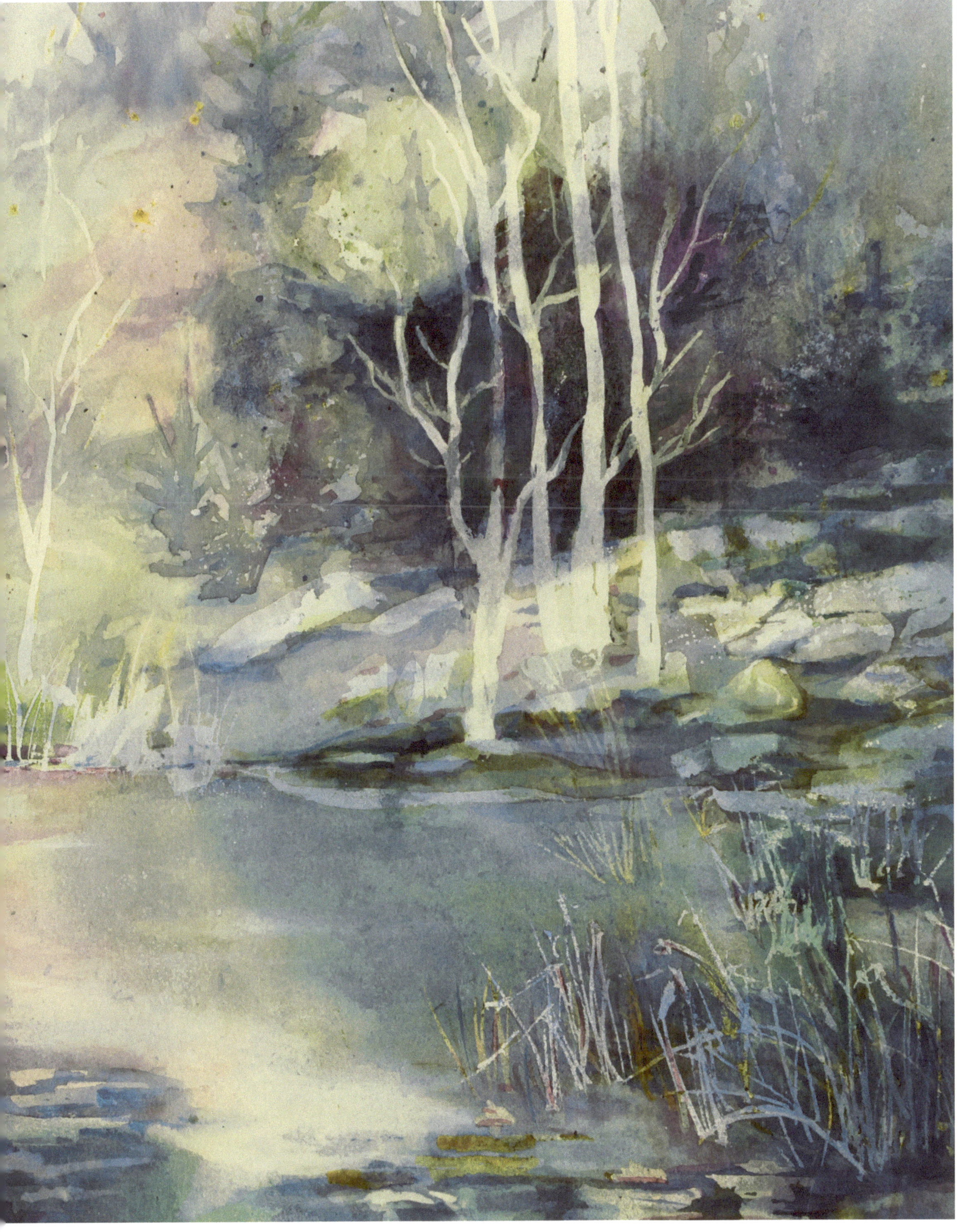

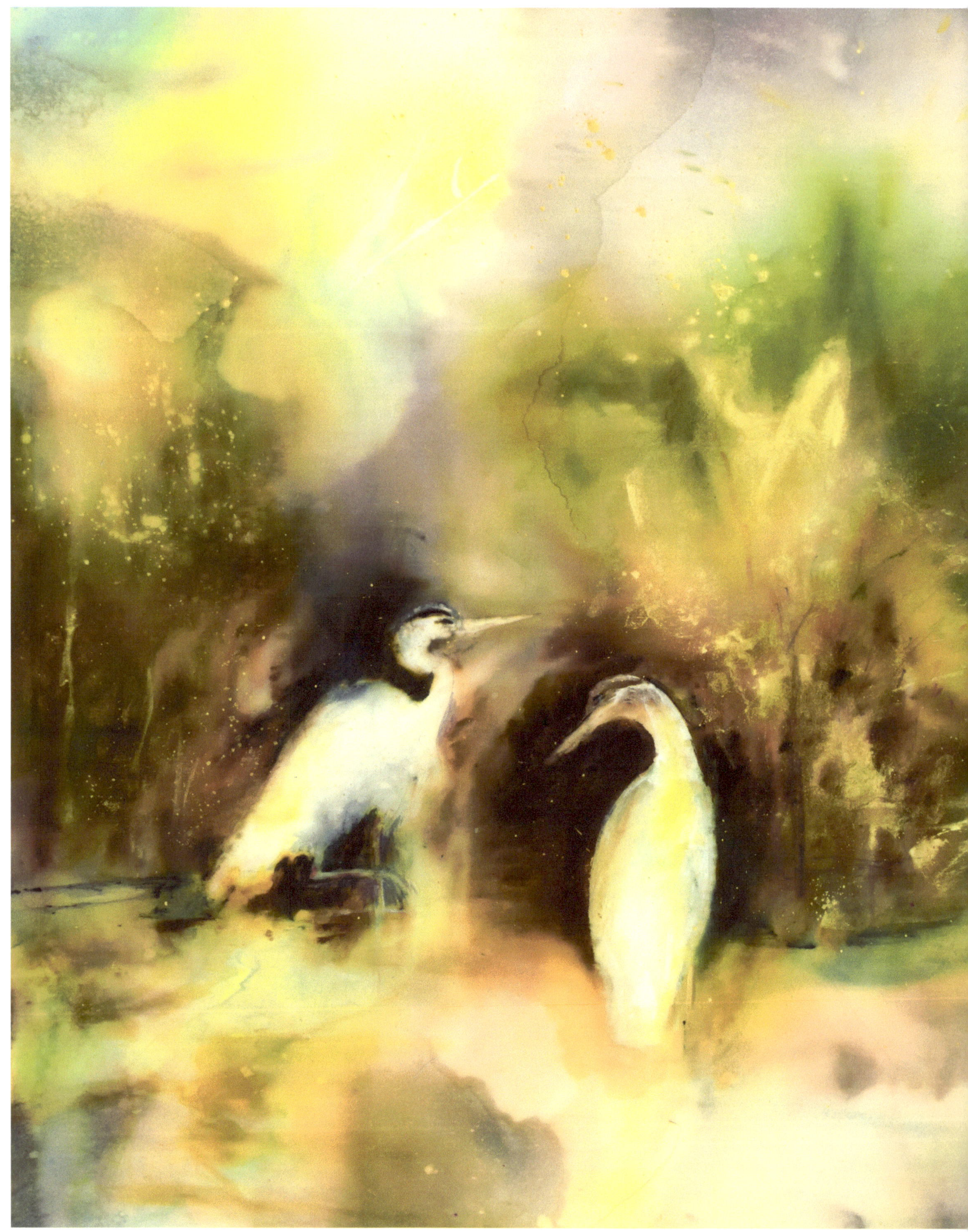

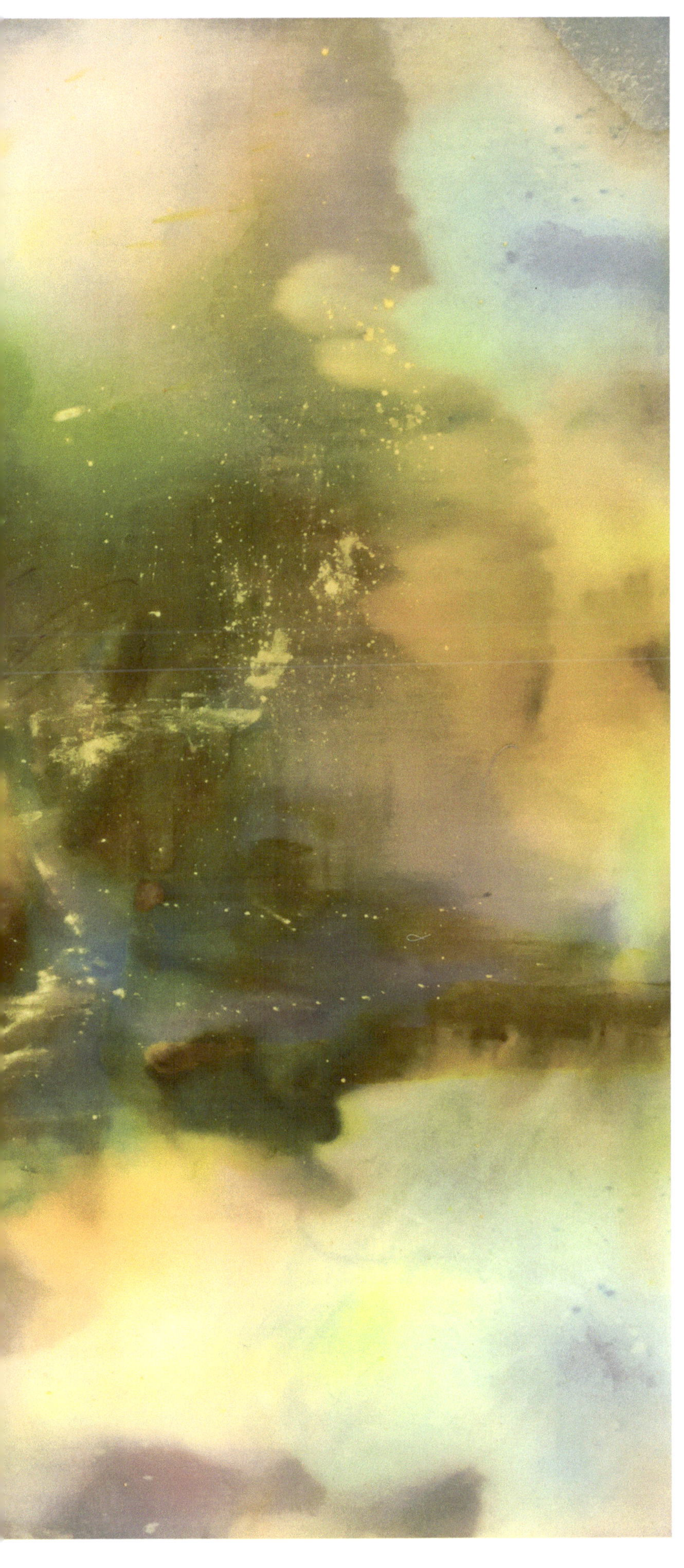

Dawn

There is us,
but there is so much more.
How will I ever know?
The child whispers.
There is no knowing.
You are only here.
Atoms we share, that spin,
that hold in gentle attraction
your heart to mine.
The great space will always exist,
the mysterious dwelling,
the mysterious home we share.

Where will you go?
The whisper is wind,
is air,
is nothing.
There is no telling for some things,
There is no wrapping in words.
Follow the long arc, hold to it still.
And still.

Materials

Much of the art presented in this book was created by painting with dyes on cotton or silk fabric. Cotton fabrics used are mercerized cotton broadcloth and cotton satin. Silks were either medium weight or sheer.

Dyes made from Procion powder pigment or Jacquard silk concentrate were applied by brush painting or spraying, similar to techniques used in watercolor work.

Dilute Chlorox bleach provided additional opportunity to lighten the pigment or create new lines and shapes after dye application. Occasionally, highlights were added with opaque Jacquard fabric acrylic paint.

Collage pieces were adhered with Super Clear or clear acrylic gel. For quilts the top layers were painted with fabric dyes, then layered with batting and backing before machine quilting. All fabrics, dyes, acrylics, and Super Clear were purchased from Dharma Trading Company.

Gemini watercolor paper (140 lb.) was used for watercolor painting. Dyes were often integrated with watercolor paints to expand the color range.

Notes on Paintings

Playful Mood

Watercolor on paper 16 x 19" (cover and title page)

Techniques in this piece were learned from Karlyn Holman early in my painting experience. The playful mood of the cover painting appropriately represents the playfulness of our process.

Egrets Anticipating the Dawn

Brush-painted with dyes on cotton fabric with gold acrylic accents, 31 x 26" (frontspiece)

Bountiful Earth

Brush-painted with dyes on cotton fabric, 17 x 21" (p.1)

Here the embryo, which emerged as a surprise during the painting process, communicates with Earth, trees, and observant shorebird.

Invitation from the Sunflower

Brush-painted with dyes and watercolor on paper, 18 x 21" (p. 2)

The image is intended to suggest the flower noticing and welcoming the bee. The earth image is in the distance. Like the first painting, it has a mysterious theme, but the "Bountiful Earth" painting is a wide-earth view and this one is a close-up intimate view of the same oneness and tender communication among all creatures.

Dance of the Gulls

Brush-painted with dyes on cotton fabric with acrylic accents, 22 x 20" (p. 4)

The white birds and ocean white caps were added to the finished painting with fabric acrylics. Ocean and marsh paintings were inspired by our time living on Tybee Island.

Butterflies in the Light of the Moon

Fabric dyes painted on silk with appliqués of dark silk and irridesdent pink threads, 22 x 31" (p. 6)

These butterfly images take on a human quality.

Dragonfly Moving Toward the Light

Brush-painted with dyes and watercolor on watercolor canvas, 12 x 16" (p. 10)

This painting started out to be a tree and ended up as a dragonfly. The techniques used in this painting were learned from Tom Lynch.

Energy in Deep Water

Brush-painted with dyes on fabric, machine quilted, 24 x 34" (p. 11)

This quilt was created for my grandson.

Tree Celebrating the Moonlight

Brush-painted with dyes on silk with appliqué, machine quilted, 25 x 32" (p. 12)

Autumn and Winter on the Mississippi

Brush-painted with dyes on cotton, machine quilted, 43 x 56" (p. 13)

The machine quilting adds flow lines to the picture, as well as new texture and depth. This scene represents my memories of the years of living near the Mississippi River in Minnesota. Techniques in this piece and many other fabric paintings were learned from Evelyn Unger.

Tree Shadows

Brush-painted with dyes on silk with appliqué and acrylic accents, 34 x 44" (p.14)

The background was painted with dyes on silk. The trees, leaves, and shadws were painted separately and appliquéd. The close-up of large leaves is contrasted with a perspective of distance in the background. Trees and their shadows stand in the mid-zone. The piece is machine-stitched on rigid backing.

Wild Gladiolas

Brush-painted with dyes on cotton fabric with French knot embroidery, machine quilted, 26 x 32" (p. 16)

This painting and the one on the next page contrast the techniques of painting flowers on fabric versus paper.

Poppies Reaching for the Light

Watercolor on paper, 18 x 25" (p. 17)

Techniques in this piece and "Grapes Ripening in View of the Wine" (*p. 20*) were learned from a workshop and books by Karlyn Holman.

Trees Resisting the Wind

Watercolor and dyes on paper, 18 x 20" (p. 18)

This piece expresses both precarious vulnerability and excitement.

Gulls Playing in the Mist

Brush-painted with dyes on cotton fabric, 19 x 26" (p. 20)

The mountain and sea background was created with dyes; the gulls and highlighted areas were created with bleach.

Egrets of Tybee Island

Watercolor and dyes on paper, 22 x 17" (p. 21)

This was painted from a photograph of a friend's backyard on Tybee Island.

Considering the Octopus

Watercolor and dyes on paper, 23 x 12" (p. 22)

This is a rather humorous painting of three fish encountering an octypus.

Tybee Island Harbor

Brush-painted with dyes on silk with appliquéd threads, 35 x 28" (p. 24)

Threads were stitched on the final painting to add movement and energy to an otherwise still scene.

Grapes Ripening in View of the Wine

Watercolor on paper, 23 x 11" (p. 27)

These vines and the poem celebrate Anneke's time in Italy.

Mountain Snowmelt

Brush-painted with dyes on cotton fabric, 26 x 32" (p. 28)

The mountains were not planned in this painting but the dye pigment moved on the wet fabric and formed their structures. This became one of the driving features of the design.

Deep Woods

Watercolor on paper, 13 x 16" (p. 29)

Techniques in this painting were learned from workshops and books by Tom Lynch.

Flowers Escaping the Vase

Watercolor on paper, 9 x 13" (p. 32)

The methods and approach used in this painting were learned from a workshop and books by Jeanne Carbonetti.

Excited Flowers

Brush-painted with dyes on paper, 13 x 22" (p. 33)

This piece combines several techniques applying watercolor, dyes, and bleach.

Flowers Awakening to a New Dawn

Brush-painted with dyes on cotton fabric, machine quilted, 24 x 36 (p. 34)

Machine quilting completed the drawing to create texture of flowers, stems and leaves.

Ancient Footprints

Brush-painted with dyes on cotton fabric, 25 x 20" (p. 36)

The design of this painting was created to complement the poem, "Footprints."

Descent of the Dragonfly

Brush-painted with dyes on cotton fabric with irridescent paint accents, 22 x 25" (p. (38)

The background images suggest forest with an emerging light of unknown source.

Butterly and the Rising Moon

Brush-painted with dyes and watercolor on cotton fabric, 27 x 26" (p. 39)

This shows the relationship of the butterfly or any insect to other life elements of Earth— the forest, flowers, mountains, and sea. During the painting a seashell emerged in the middle of the butterfly and the mountains moved down through the wings.

Peace and Turbulence Among the Trees

Brush-painted with dyes on cotton fabric, 34 x 22" (p. 40)

Birds Circling Mountain Glacier

Watercolor and dyes on paper, 21 x 18" (p. 42)

In this painting the birds emerged as a surprise in the structure of the mountains. Others were then added and accented to complete the piece.

Playful Fish

Brush-painted with dyes on cotton fabric with acrylic accents, 18 x 19" (p. 44)

Egret Noticing the Fish

Brush-painted with dyes on cotton fabric with acrylic accents and added fibers, 14 x 16" (p. 45)

Here the egret considers the fish below, while on the facing page, the fish go on complacently playing deep below the ocean surface.

Gulls in the Light of the Ocean

Brush-painted with dyes and acrylics on cotton fabric, 27 x 19" (p. 46)

Trees Reaching for Each Other

Brush-painted with dyes and watercolors on cotton fabric, 18 x 25" (p. 48)

The trees on the right reach out to those across the path, while the yellow tree becomes interwoven with the background trees. These symbolic images are meant to express communication that I believe exists among all creatures, even plants.

Feeding the Quartet

Watercolor and dyes on paper, 12 x 18". (p. 50)

Secret Life of Butterflies

Collage: organza silk and paper, 28 x 31" (p. 51)

These two facing pages show a contrast between watercolor on paper and a fabric collage. Depth, feeling, and intimacy are achieved in both, but with very different techniques.

Earth Communicating with Nature Spirits

Collage: Brush-painted with dyes and acrylics on paper with dyed tissue paper, 22 x 16". (p. 52)

In this piece I tried to show macro, expansive earth views, together with the more intimate detail.

Peaceful Reflections

Watercolor on paper, 20 x 18". (p. 54)

This painting was inspired by our backyard pond and painted for my son, Chris.

Coming of the Trees

Brush-painted with dyes and watercolor on cotton fabric, 18 x 19" (p. 56)

The red trees at the left were painted primarily with watercolor, while the rest of the painting was completed with dyes. The circle in the upper middle represents Earth.

Flowers Appreciating the Water

Brush-painted with dyes on cotton fabric with unryu paper accent, 18 x 19" (p. 57)

Unryu was applied tn the upper right on the central the flower to provide contrast in color and texture. The background images beside the flowers suggest bodies of water.

Unity

Collage: Watercolor painting on paper with dyed paper and organza, 23 x 19" (p. 58)

Here the light passes through Earth and into the ocean flow as trees, rocks, and marsh grass appear.

Fog Settles Softly on the River

Watercolor and dyes on paper, 24 x 22" (p. 60)

Egrets Anticipating the Dawn

Brush-painted with dyes on cotton fabric with gold acrylic accents, 31 x 26" (p. 62)

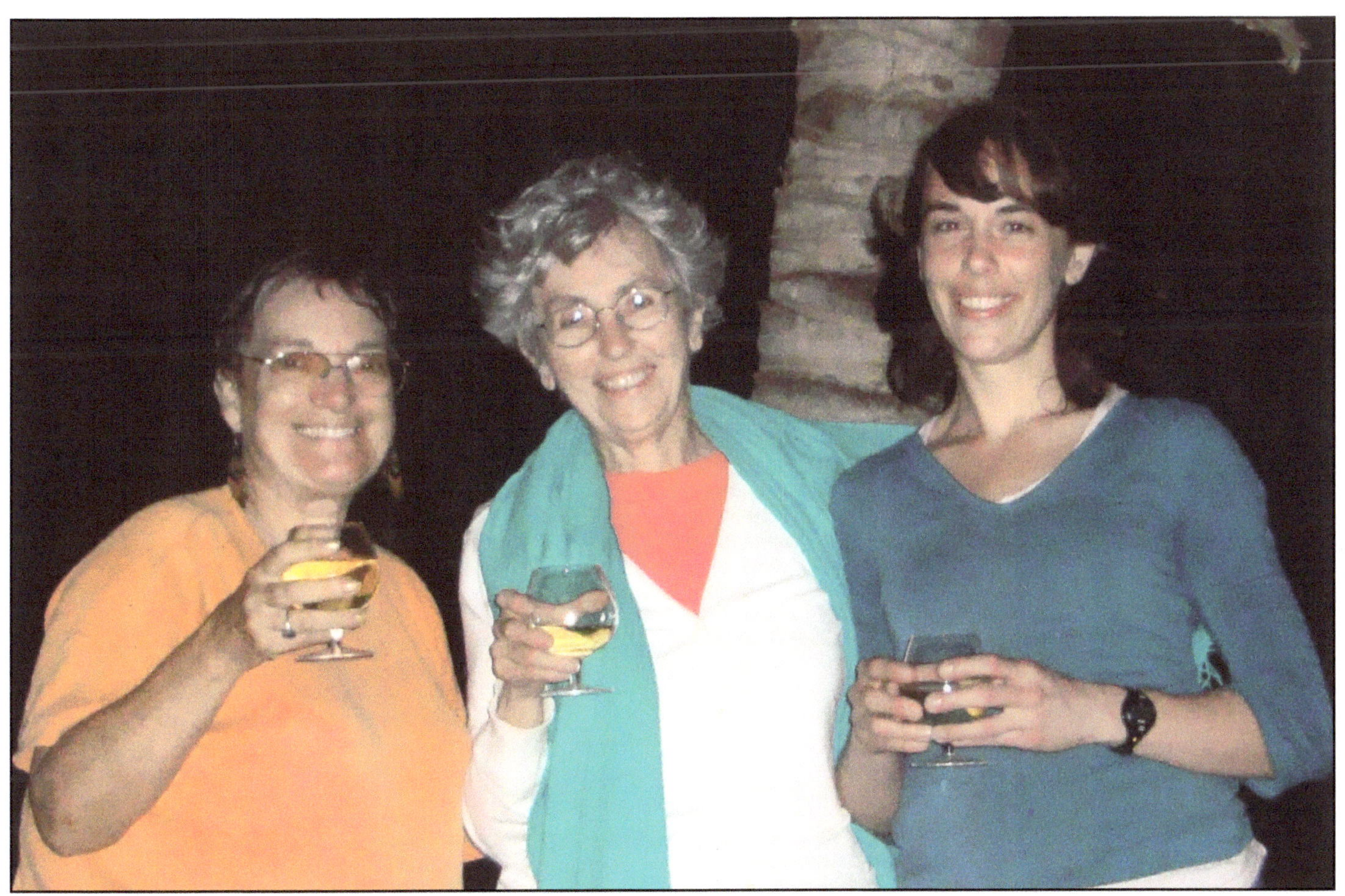

Judy Lumb (Editor, *Producciones de la Hamaca*), Judy Bender, and Anneke Bender

www.ingramcontent.com/pod-product-compliance
Lightning Source LLC
LaVergne TN
LVHW070509120826
845147LV00031BA/300
9789768142276